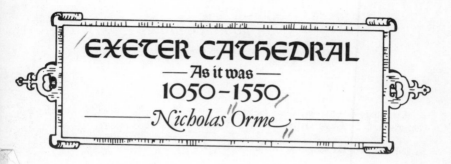

EXETER CATHEDRAL
— As it was —
1050 – 1550
Nicholas Orme

DEVON BOOKS

Non nobis Domine

First published 1986 by Devon Books
Copyright © Nicholas Orme, 1986

British Library Cataloguing in Publication Data

Orme, Nicholas
    Exeter Cathedral as it was 1050-1550.
    1. Exeter Cathedral—History
    I. Title
    942.3'56   DA690.E9

    ISBN 0-86114-785-5

DEVON BOOKS
Publishers to the Devon County Council
Devon Books is a division of A. Wheaton & Co. Ltd which represents:

Design, Editorial & Publicity
Production & Manufacturing
A. Wheaton & Co. Ltd, Hennock Road, Exeter EX2 8RP
Tel: 0392-74121 Telex: 42749 (WHEATN G)
(A. Wheaton & Co. Ltd is a member of the BPCC Group)

Sales & Distribution
Town & Country Books, 24 Priory Avenue, Kingskerswell,
Newton Abbot, TQ12 5AQ. Tel: 08047-2690

Contents

List of Illustrations

Preface

Exeter Cathedral is known and loved, in its present form, by many thousands of people. But what was it like in earlier times? Why was it built in the first place? How did it look, inside and out, when it was finished in the fourteenth century? Who were its clergy, worshippers and visitors? What happened there on ordinary days, and at special times of the year? This book sets out to answer these questions. It falls into three parts: the first describes what the Close and the cathedral looked like in the Middle Ages; the second considers the people involved with the place – the clergy, the king and the general public; and the third explains what went on in the building – the pattern of the day, the major events of the year and the worship of the saints. The final chapter shows how, in the sixteenth century, the Reformation changed all this, bringing the Middle Ages to an end as far as Exeter Cathedral was concerned.

I have received much generous assistance in writing this book. First and foremost, Mrs A. M. Erskine, Cathedral Archivist, has for many years given me invaluable help in producing documents and discussing problems; my second and fourth chapters owe a good deal to her published work. I am also grateful to Mr P. W. Thomas, Assistant Cathedral Librarian; to Mr J. Allan, Dr A. E. Goodman, Dr J. H. Harvey and Mr D. Lepine for providing useful information, and to Mr S. Goddard for photographing three of the plates and for his skill and patience in drawing the maps and plans. The Dean and Chapter of Exeter Cathedral, the Royal Albert Memorial Museum, Exeter, and Dr D. Portman have all kindly given permission for the reproduction of illustrations, My wife, who married me in the cathedral, has nobly borne with living in its shadow ever since.

Nicholas Orme
Brampford Speke
February 1986

v

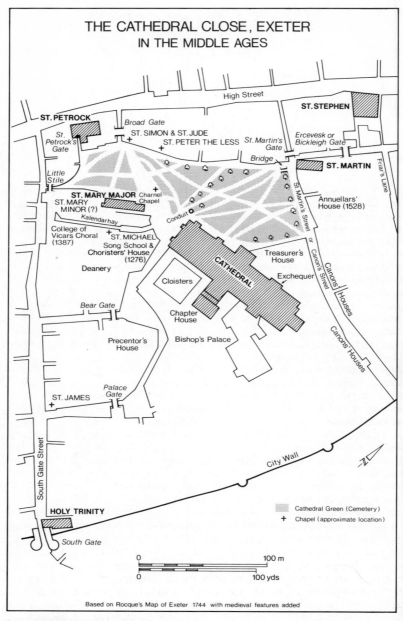

THE CATHEDRAL CLOSE, EXETER
IN THE MIDDLE AGES

High Street

ST. STEPHEN

ST. PETROCK

Broad Gate

St.
Petrock's
Gate

ST. SIMON & ST. JUDE
ST. PETER THE LESS

St. Martin's
Gate

Ercevesk or
Bickleigh Gate

Little
Stile

Bridge

ST. MARTIN

Friar's Lane

ST. MARY MAJOR Charnel
ST. MARY   Chapel
MINOR (?)

Annuellars'
House (1528)

Kalendarhay

Conduit

College of
Vicars Choral
(1387)

ST. MICHAEL
Song School &
Choristers' House
(1276)

St. Martin's Street or Canon's Street

Treasurer's
House

Deanery

CATHEDRAL

Exchequer

Cloisters

Canons' Houses

Bear Gate

Chapter
House

Precentor's
House

Bishop's Palace

Canons' Houses

Palace
Gate

ST. JAMES

South Gate Street

City Wall

HOLY TRINITY

░░░ Cathedral Green (Cemetery)

+ Chapel (approximate location)

South Gate

```
0                    100 m
0                    100 yds
```

Based on Rocque's Map of Exeter 1744 with medieval features added

The Cathedral Close, Exeter

1

The Close

A good way to revisit the cathedral as it was in the Middle Ages is to walk towards it down St Martin's Lane, between The Ship Inn and The Royal Clarence Hotel. There are at least eight other routes to the cathedral, each with a charm of its own, but this lane, more than most, conveys a feeling of what Exeter was like 600 years ago. A narrow street just wide enough for a cart, it is hemmed in by lofty buildings as the side-streets were in the Middle Ages, when 5000 people crowded into the 98 acres of the old walled city. It is also a dramatic street, which gradually unfolds a spectacle. As you advance, the walls appear to draw apart, like the curtains of a theatre. A green and spacious vista opens before you. Left, the profiles of the canons' houses stretch away towards the east. Right, the successors of medieval tenements curve westwards into the distance. Ahead there is a wide stretch of grass and trees, and beyond the trees the whole length of the cathedral, brown, grey and massive against the rose-red brick and sandstone of the rest of the city.

The open space around the cathedral is the Close. Let us imagine what it was like in the fourteenth century, when the present cathedral was built.[1] The elements of the Close are the same today as they were then, but there have been many changes of detail. In those days, the grass which is nowadays merely a place for sitting or strolling on was the chief burial-ground of the city. The local monasteries and friaries had their own cemeteries for burying their clergy and, very occasionally, other people. But, unlike most churches, the Exeter parish churches did not possess churchyards for burial. Instead, the cathedral acted as the parish church of the city for funerals and burials. Every layman and woman who died in Exeter had to be taken to the cathedral for their funeral and (unless they got a special exemption) buried in the cathedral cemetery.[2] The cathedral authorities, the dean and chapter, guarded this privilege jealously. Not only did it give their church extra status in the city, but it brought in a good deal of money. People who went to funerals made offerings, bought candles to burn round the corpse, and often paid for the ringing of bells.[3] Even the grave cost sixpence, which the cathedral 'pitmaker' or sexton charged for digging it.[4] You could get permission from the dean and chapter to be buried in the monastic cemeteries, but in all cases save for monks and friars, the funeral service before the burial had to take place in the

1

cathedral. Only the richer citizens and their wives generally went to the trouble of being buried anywhere else. Until the 1630s, the great majority were laid to rest beside the cathedral. By that time the cemetery could no longer cope with the number of burials, and the bishop, Joseph Hall, complained that the accumulation of corpses and the mounds of earth above them threatened to bury the cathedral itself. Accordingly, in 1637, the dean and chapter agreed with the mayor and corporation that a new graveyard should be opened in Bartholomew Street, and gave £150 towards the cost.[5] The cathedral green was levelled and became, as it is now, simply a pleasant area of grass.

We can obtain a good idea of the green's appearance in the later Middle Ages from a 'plat' or bird's-eye-view of the Close which was drawn for John Hooker, the Exeter town clerk and historian, towards the end of the sixteenth century.[6] Until the 1830s, the grass did not extend as far south as it does now, because a long building – the treasurer's house – projected from the north tower of the cathedral towards the nearby road. The marks of the gable of this house can still be seen imprinted on the tower. Despite this fact, the grassy area remained quite large, and it was criss-crossed by about a dozen paths, several more than there are today. Each autumn drifts of leaves fell on the grass and graves from elm trees planted round the outer edges of the green. Eighteen trees are shown on Hooker's map. According to the citizens of Exeter in the middle of the sixteenth century, the trees were planted in 1286 to mark the boundary between the cemetery and the streets of the Close.[7] They were certainly there by the 1380s, when it is said that people had illegally felled some of the timber,[8] and they lasted until the early sixteenth century, when they gradually disappeared through natural decay and human action. Elderly men recalled in 1554 that eight trees were cut down in 1497 so that Henry VII could stand at a window in the treasurer's house and see the Cornish rebels drawn up on the grass to receive his pardon. Soon after this, a large elm by St Petrock's Church was blown down in a gale, and the rest of the trees did not survive much longer. By the 1510s they were 'hollow and great' and had become the lurking-places of 'evil and naughty persons' who threatened the peace and order of the Close. Dr Richard More, the treasurer, who was responsible for the upkeep of the cemetery, accordingly got the bishop's permission to have the trees destroyed, and this was done in 1516–17.[9] For the rest of the sixteenth century, the Close was largely bare of trees, and their inclusion on Hooker's map is a piece of historical reconstruction, not a statement of fact with regard to his own times.

Not all the Close was a cemetery, however, even in those days. There were streets and houses, and domestic life went on beside the graves and sometimes even among them. Two streets ran down the east and north sides of the cemetery, as they do today, and others crossed it: one from St Martin's Church to the cathedral (now a tarmacked path) and a second from Broad Gate to the bishop's palace. The only street with a name was St Martin's Street or Canon Street, which ran along the eastern side, but all four streets were highways and, like the streets of the city, came under the authority of the mayor and corporation.

The outer edges of the Close were fringed by houses. In all those along St

2

Martin's Street lived canons and other cathedral clergy; behind them were yards and gardens stretching to a back lane called Friars' Lane (now Chapel Street). On the north side, where there are shops today, there were no house-fronts in the later Middle Ages, only the backs of houses in the High Street. They were not allowed to have an entrance into the Close, for reasons which will become clear presently. The west side of the Close contained another group of clergymen's houses, notably the deanery, the precentor's house, the bishop's palace, and various smaller houses of lesser clergy. There was a special water-supply for the Close, separate from that of the city. The water was brought by underground passages to a conduit by the north-west corner of the cathedral nave. On Hooker's map the conduit is shown as a little round building like a well-house; by his time water was piped from it to several of the canons' houses. The houses in the Close on Hooker's map look like the houses in the rest of the city, but there was a basic difference between their inhabitants. Everyone who lived in the Close was either a cleric or a cleric's servant, and all were male. Women came and went through the Close by day, but none of them (apart from very important visitors) ever lawfully stayed inside it overnight.[10]

There were churches and chapels in the Close as well as houses. When the present cathedral began to be built, in about 1270, the Close included seven other religious buildings, so that the queen of the city had, as it were, a bevy of ladies-in-waiting.[11] In the twelfth and thirteenth centuries Exeter possessed a surprisingly large number of churches and chapels to cater for its population: some thirty for 5000 people, excluding monasteries and friaries. They were located in most of the major streets and also outside the walls, but were particularly thick on the ground in the Close, along the sides which bordered on the High Street and South Street. Moving from east to west you would have passed the churches of St Martin, St Peter the Less, St Simon and St Jude, St Petrock, St Mary Minor, St Mary Major and St Michael. Some had perhaps been founded by lords for their tenants, others by groups of people, on a voluntary basis, and it is probable that some of them drew their congregations from all over the city, rather than from specific areas. Then, in 1222, Exeter was divided into parishes of a modern kind, and all the major churches were allocated territories near by to control. This caused problems for the chapels in the Close, because it was not possible to give them all sufficient houses and inhabitants to support them. In the long term only three became parochial and survived: St Martin's and St Petrock's, which still exist, and St Mary Major, which was demolished in 1971. St Michael's was appropriated by the dean as his private chapel and can still be seen on the north side of the ancient deanery. The other three disappeared between about 1260 and 1300. There has been a good deal of conjecture about the church of St Mary Minor, which is sometimes imagined to be an alternative name for St Mary Steps. The records, how-ever, leave no doubt that it stood very close to the church of St Mary Major, perhaps on the west side,[12] and was united to the latter in 1285.[13]

As we accustom ourselves to the Close as it was between 1270 and 1550, we must get used to something which is likely to come as a shock: the mess. Nowadays the grass is mown, the paths are tarmacked and the streets are paved and walled. Only the visitors are untidy. In the past, the Close was

3

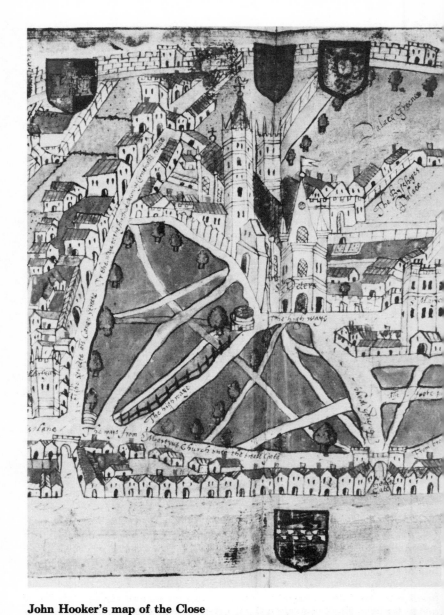

John Hooker's map of the Close
The earliest picture of the Close and cathedral. By no means accurate in every detail, it nevertheless shows interesting features: the gates, green, paths, trees, conduit and bridge.

dirtier and more disorderly. An open ditch appears to have run between St Martin's Street and the cemetery (Hooker's map depicts a little bridge by St Martin's Church that probably crossed it). This carried refuse from the canons' houses to the city walls.[14] The green itself was worn away by paths, which have an unpaved unofficial look on Hooker's map and must have been dusty in summer, muddy in winter. The grass between the paths was not serene and meadow-like but scarred with recent graves.

Burials were so frequent that no one could expect to occupy a space for ever, and the graves were dug over again sooner or later, as Yorick's grave in *Hamlet* is reopened for Ophelia after a dozen years or so. The bones disturbed by the pitmaker, and those that rose to the surface, were gathered up and put in a charnel-house. This house stood in the west part of the Close, near the church of St Mary Major,[15] and consisted of two storeys: a chapel above, with an outside pulpit for open-air sermons, and the charnel proper beneath, where loose bones were stacked up. The building was destroyed at the Reformation, in the 1550s or 1560s.[16] The frequency with which graves were redug, in addition to the poverty of most of their occupants, may be the reason why we do not hear of gravestones in the cemetery, and why none is shown on Hooker's map. People remembered where graves were, because they sometimes asked to be buried beside their spouse or their parents, but the sites do not appear to have been marked. Only the wealthy, who paid to be buried inside the cathedral or in other local churches, left permanent memorials of themselves in the form of inscribed stones or monumental brasses.

Not only was the cemetery scruffy, it was disfigured by secular activities which we would not think at all suitable for consecrated ground. Games were played among the graves, for some people have always regarded the Close as a recreation area. The authorities apparently tolerated this, since games were forbidden only near the buildings, where there was a risk of damage to walls or windows.[17] Even the clergy joined in, and when John Forn got into trouble in 1386 for playing a game with laymen in the cemetery, the fact that he was playing seems to have mattered less than his absence from cathedral matins![18] Piles of filth and rubble lay about the Close, thrown out of the canons' houses or dumped by citizens; timber was piled up there, bonfires were made,[19] animals roamed about and trading went on. In the fourteenth century there even seems to have been a fish market, near the Broad Gate, though it disappeared later.[20] In 1374 the bishop, Thomas Brantingham, felt it necessary to order the clearance of timber, dung and filth. In 1386 he prohibited timber-stacking for a second time, and also trading. In 1389 he again forbade the deposit of human and animal refuse.[21] The easy-going Robert Brok, cathedral treasurer from 1377 to 1388, was partly to blame for this, because he was responsible for looking after the Close. His fellow canons claimed that while Brok was treasurer workmen laboured in the cemetery, timber was stacked there by outsiders, trees were felled, pigs came into the Close, horses browsed on the grass, and strangers offered goods for sale. The treasurer did not deny the charges, but he said he was not to blame. True, people worked in the cemetery, but against his orders. Those concerned were not under his jurisdiction, and if he were to expel them by force, he would have to turn his hand to war. As for the horses, the treasurer neatly turned this point against his opponents. The horses were there because they brought carts to the canons' houses. If the canons would provide them with fodder, the horses would not cause trouble by grazing in the Close. He ended his defence lightheartedly, with some rhyming verses in Latin; in translation:

> If you love your guest, feed his mare with the best;
> You throw all to the air if you do not feed the mare![22]

The Close, then, was by no means the haven of tranquillity the name suggests today. On the contrary, it was the frontier between the cathedral and the city, the sacred and the secular, and experienced some of the strife and lawlessness of a march or border of a medieval kingdom. Even today the green is consecrated ground and has to be protected against unseemly behaviour. In the Middle Ages, however, the special character of the Close was more pronounced and needed more defence. It will seem odd, in view of the untidiness of the cemetery, that its consecrated nature was taken much more seriously than it is now. The slightest spilling of blood was reckoned to pollute its sacred status. It only needed a fight to break out and someone to be wounded, or simply to get a bloody nose, for the cemetery to be closed immediately until it had been reconsecrated by the bishop.[23] Then again, the Close was a privileged area at law, a city within the city. It formed part of a separate jurisdiction called the 'bishop's fee' or 'St Stephen's fee', over which the mayor and corporation, to their annoyance, had virtually no authority.[24] They could patrol the streets of the Close, but had no power over the cathedral, the cemetery, the clergy, their houses, or their servants. This situation was not peculiar to Exeter. It was the same in other cities where there were strong bodies of clergy, most notably in the university towns of Oxford and Cambridge. Wherever it existed, the system caused trouble. City corporations resented the clergy's privileges and tried to undermine them. In Exeter the city authorities periodically attempted to make arrests within the Close and to send in their coroners to view dead bodies there. This is not surprising, given that criminals often fled from the city to the Close to take sanctuary, and some of the breaches of privilege took place during hot pursuit by the city officers. Other criminals came to the Close not to escape but to rob and attack the clergy, and it was hard to keep such people out. The cathedral community was not a monastery that could shut itself off from the world on its own terms. It occupied a sector of an important city, close to the city's heart, and there was no way of controlling absolutely who came and went between the two areas.

The most sensational breach of the Close by laymen was the murder of the precentor in 1283.[25] The background to this deed was a quarrel between the bishop, Peter Quinil, and a cleric named John Pycot who had got himself elected dean of the cathedral in somewhat dubious circumstances. Quinil refused to recognise Pycot as dean and set out to remove him, but Pycot was an Exeter man with various supporters in the city, including the mayor, Alured de la Porte. The precentor of the cathedral, Walter de Lechlade, was one of the bishop's henchmen and seems to have been regarded by Pycot's faction as a major opponent. Accordingly, some of them resolved to eliminate him. On 10 November 1283, at about midnight,

Lechlade left his house (the Chantry, now the Cathedral School) to walk to the cathedral for the night service of matins. A signal of this fact was taken by a servant of Alured called Thomas the Leader to the city's South Gate, which, by pre-arrangement, was open. Thomas blew a horn and a group of conspirators emerged from hiding and entered the city. When the precentor came out of the cathedral with two or three of his servants at about 1.30 a.m., the ruffians struck him down near the entrance to his house, and killed him. In due course the dead man's relative, John de Lechlade, instituted legal proceedings against Pycot, Alured and nineteen other people, both clergy and laity. The case was slow to proceed and at one stage John himself was imprisoned for failing to prove his accusations. In the end, however, the bishop approached the king about the matter, and in December 1285 Edward I arrived in Exeter to settle the case in person. From Christmas Eve till 28 December, with the exception of Christmas Day, the king's judges tried the accused men in the castle, in the presence of the king himself. Five laymen were found guilty and executed immediately by hanging; they included the mayor, the porter of the South Gate and Thomas the Leader. The clergy were luckier; they were handed over to their bishops to be dealt with and suffered lesser penalties. Pycot himself was deprived of the deanery and retired into a monastery. As so often in these cases, it seems that the actual murderers escaped.

The murder of the precentor had a long-term importance. On 1 January 1286, as soon as the trials were over, the king gave permission for the Close to be surrounded by a high wall and a series of gates, to protect the clergy at night.[26] The sites and sizes of the gates were settled by an agreement between the clergy and the laity three months later. Seven gates were put up. Clockwise from west to north, they were: Bishop's or Palace Gate, Bear Gate, Little Stile, St Petrock's Gate, Broad or Fishfold Gate, St Martin's Gate and Ercevesk or Bickleigh (later St Katherine's) Gate. Two of the gates – Little Stile and St Petrock's – were merely posterns for pedestrians; Bear Gate and Ercevesk Gate were eight feet wide and could admit pack-horses, and the other three were wide enough for carts.[27] The principal entrance to the Close became Broad Gate, between the Guildhall and the west front of the cathedral. This was and still is the entry for visiting dignitaries: mayors, bishops and royalty. The gates were open by day and shut at night. A porter of the Close was appointed to supervise them, with a house on or near Broad Gate itself. Being a member of the cathedral clergy, he was well placed to provide security for his fellow clerics.[28] Walls were constructed between the gates, where access was not already prevented by buildings, and linked at each end to the city walls. Lay people with houses adjoining the Close were made to block up their back entrances.[29] From this time onwards, the cathedral precinct became a true close, a closed-in place, and it remained so till the gates were taken away in the early nineteenth century. There are still posts at Broad Gate and St Martin's Gate which show where the gates used to be.

The new defences protected the Close at night, but they did nothing to solve the problems of contact between the clergy and the laity during the day. There was still plenty of opportunity for breaches of the peace and disputes with the city authorities, and these were particularly numerous in the 1440s, when the bishop, Edmund Lacy, and the mayor, John Shillingford, each appealed against the other to the king's chancellor in London. The papers which the two sides submitted on this occasion are still extant in the form of the so-called 'Shillingford Letters', and they vividly convey the sense of grievance which each side felt.[30] The mayor and corporation complained that they were excluded from their just rights in the Close. They could not gain proper access to the city wall in order to inspect and repair it, or to the cloister garth where some of their relatives were buried. The clergy encroached on the streets of the Close by building stairs and extending gardens; they choked the drains with rubbish, causing floods to rise behind the Close, and some of them came out of the Close at night to Beaufitz Tavern near Broad Gate, where they woke the citizens with noise and brawling.

The clergy replied by pointing to the breaches of the peace committed by the citizens. It had been necessary to shut the cloister because of damage caused by people playing games — 'the toppe, queke, penny prykke and worst [of all] atte tenys' — which fouled the cloister walls and broke the windows. The city authorities had entered the Close illegally and tried to arrest people over whom they had no power. John Vouslegh, servant of the cathedral chancellor, was seized near the bishop's palace while he was holding the skirts of his master's cope up out of the dust during the Ascension Day procession. Hugh Lucas, one of the bishop's tenants and therefore outside city jurisdiction, was chased into the cathedral itself by sergeants carrying 'swords, daggers and other invasive weapons' while a service was in progress. This resulted in a pitched battle. Despite the service, several clergy came out of the choir, in the words of the city, with 'swords, custels, long knives and Irish skenes drawn in their hands, to have slain the said sergeants'. Blows were exchanged, and the city officers 'scarcely escaped out of the church with their lives'. As for Lucas, he evaded capture, undeservedly, for he was no innocent victim but a notorious trouble-maker.

Relations between the clergy and the citizens, therefore, were sometimes warlike, but it would be wrong to imply that they were always or only so. For much, and probably most, of the time the city and the cathedral got on harmoniously and even amicably. At an official level, in particular, the disputes seem rather like the confrontations between modern politicians; they were rituals which observed well-defined limits. Many of the clergy and the citizens belonged to the same families, and others were personal friends. John Shillingford, who led the city's fight in the 1440s, was a blood relation of two former cathedral canons. When he needed to appoint trustees of his property, he chose five of the cathedral clergy, and two others acted as the executors of his will, one them being Henry Webber, who had been one of his chief clerical opponents.[31] A century later John Hooker was an equally redoubtable defender of the city and its rights against the clergy, and wrote a good deal on the subject. Yet he was the godson of the cathedral treasurer, he knew many of the canons, and in 1584 he became the first man ever to publish a history of the cathedral and its bishops.[32] The clergy, for their part, respected the city's governors. The mayor was prayed for publicly on Sundays, and he received a daily allowance of bread from the cathedral as if he were one of the canons.[33] By the sixteenth century, mayors regularly attended the cathedral in state and had the privilege of hearing mass, said by their own chaplain, in a side-chapel. In short, the quarrels were part of a complex relationship which veered from conflict to friendship, but was usually peaceful and in general stable. Both sides were Exonians, after all. Hooker summed it up in 1584, in words which are still appropriate today, 'There is,' he said, 'a sympathy and affinity between this city and the church, both of which are enclosed and environed within one wall.' Though they are 'in certain privileges distinguished', they have so much in common that they 'be, as it were, one body'.[34]

2

The Cathedral

When we turn from the green of the Close to the stones of the cathedral, two of the building's attributes are likely to spring to mind: its age and its beauty. You may not think that it is beautiful, and prefer to call it curious, or even (concurring with the opinion of the late Sir John Betjeman) disappointing, but it is hard not to be struck by the cathedral's antiquity. It is, after all, over 600 years old. What did people think of the building when it was new, in the fourteenth and fifteenth centuries? The answer is that they probably felt the same emotions as we do. There can be little doubt that those who built the cathedral, and many of its early visitors, regarded it as a fine building. Bishop Brantingham, encouraging donations to the fabric in 1391, talked of its 'decor' – its beauty or decorousness – and its glory.[1] William Worcester, the first English 'tourist' to have left us a record of his thoughts, wrote in 1478 of the 'beautiful lights' of the windows and 'the most beautiful way' in which the church was vaulted over inside.[2] To such people the cathedral had a freshness which it has now lost, but it also had a past, as even they soon realized. The building they saw was not the first to occupy the site, but the third. The two great towers and part of the nave survived from its Norman predecessor, and there were relics, tombs and books from the Saxon period before that. The cathedral was historic as an institution even when it was new as a building.

Medieval Exonians were conscious of their history and proud of it. The citizens believed that their city had existed before the Romans came to Britain, and that its origins were lost in the mists of time. The early history of Exeter, like that of Britain in general, was invented by Geoffrey of Monmouth in the twelfth century. His *Historia Regum Britanniae* was an immense success and convinced most of its readers. Geoffrey tells how, shortly after Christ's Ascension, Vespasian and the Romans besieged Exeter, then called Kaerpenhuelgoit, 'the city on the high wooded hill'. The British king Arviragus, son of Cymbeline, brought an army to relieve the city and Vespasian made peace and sailed away.[3] In the fifteenth century it was believed that Vespasian went from Britain to the Holy Land and sacked Jerusalem, selling thirty Jews' heads for a penny. Exeter stood when Jerusalem fell: a fine piece of civic ingenuity![4]

The clergy too were interested in history. In the 1440s, a chronicle written on a 'table' (some kind of board) was displayed in the cathedral choir; this was the earliest cathedral guide-book. It was a short history of

Broad Gate in 1822
Frowning on passers-by, the Broad Gate was the chief of the seven gates which defended the Close against the city. Until removed in 1825, it was also the entrance for kings and bishops.

the world with special reference to Exeter, including Vespasian's visit, the foundation of the cathedral in 1050, and the dates of all the bishops of Exeter down to recent times. Being written in Latin, the chronicle was intended mainly for clerics, but it was also read by some educated lay people. William Worcester took notes from it on his visit, and the corporation of Exeter quoted from it to justify their claim to authority over the cathedral Close. The 'table' was still there in the late sixteenth century, but it had not been brought up to date and this inspired the city chamberlain, John Hooker, to enlarge and extend it as his *Catalog of Bishops* in 1584: the first modern history of the cathedral in English. The Latin chronicle is thus the direct ancestor of all the books and guides which help the scholar and the visitor today.[5]

In a sense the cathedral was never wholly new. Even when it was founded in 1050, it took over the buildings and possessions of an earlier monastery. The monastery may date back as far as the year 670, a date quoted in some fabricated charters of the late eleventh century, and there is a reliable reference to *an* early monastery in Exeter in the biography of St Boniface by Willibald, written in about the 760s. St Boniface was born Wynfrith, the son of Anglo-Saxon parents, in the south of England, and Willibald's Life describes how he was brought up as a boy in a monastery at 'Escancastre' under an abbot named Wulfhard in about the 680s.[6] Boniface, a great missionary in Germany and organizer of the German Church, was martyred at Dokkum in Holland in 754. He is the earliest known saint to be associated with Exeter and one of its most famous sons, although he spent only a few years of his childhood in the city. Despite his later achievements, no memories of him survived in Exeter, and it was not until the fourteenth century that somebody rediscovered his local connection. That person was Bishop Grandisson.

In 1337 Grandisson drew up his Ordinal, which will be often mentioned in this book, defining how cathedral services were to be carried out. In the service for St Boniface's Day (5 June), he provided lessons to be read at matins which stated for the first time that Boniface was born at Crediton and went on to repeat the assertion of Willibald that the saint was brought up in the monastery at Exeter.[7] There is no previous evidence linking Boniface with Crediton, and this appears to have been an idea of Grandisson's own, based upon grounds which are not now clear to us. It did not strike a chord with the people of Devon. Grandisson apparently set up an altar of St Boniface in Crediton church; this is mentioned once in the records in 1334 but never referred to again, and although the story of Boniface's life would have been read at cathedral matins every 5 June until the Reformation, there was no cult of him in Exeter: no relics, statue or altar.[8] He did not even figure in the cathedral chronicle. He has only recently become popular in Devon and the dedication of a chapel to him in the cathedral is an equally modern invention.

We do not know the subsequent history of Boniface's monastery, and it is not until the tenth century that things begin to grow clearer.[9] In 909 or thereabouts, Devon and Cornwall were separated from the diocese of Sherborne and given a bishop of their own, with his seat at Crediton. A little later King Athelstan (925–939) founded a new monastery in Exeter or refounded the old one. Technically, he probably founded a minster, staffed by clerics who were not true monks, rather than a monastery proper. The evidence for the foundation is not contemporary. The earliest surviving record appeared a hundred years or more after Athelstan's death in a group of six charters fabricated by the cathedral to establish claims to lands which it held in the late eleventh century.[10] The charters are bad, indeed incredible, forgeries, five of them dating Athelstan's grant to A.D. 670, 250 years too early, while the other, though dated 937, seems to have been copied from a charter of Abingdon Abbey. But there is no reason to doubt the tradition they enshrine: that Athelstan was a generous benefactor and probably a refounder of the Exeter monastery, which from this period onwards occupied the same premises and some of the same property as the future cathedral. In later years the cathedral clergy looked back to Athelstan as their first historic figure, even as their 'first founder', forgetting Boniface and the earlier monastery. An obit (anniversary mass) was celebrated annually on the day of his death (27 October), the cathedral's relics were believed to have been given by him, and the coat of arms ascribed to him can still be seen in the great east window and elsewhere.[11] The site of his minster has been plausibly identified as lying west of the present cathedral, beneath the later church of St Mary Major.[12] The minster seems to have had a prosperous history in the tenth century — King Edgar is said to have put in monks in 968 — until the Danes ravaged Exeter in 1003. According to a grant of King Cnut in 1119, the monastery's records were destroyed by fire during an attack by heathens, and no doubt much else suffered too. After this, the church probably reverted to being a minster again, with a less ambitious kind of clerical life.

When Leofric became Bishop of Devon and Cornwall in 1046, the bishop's seat was still at Crediton. Leofric was a reformer, and Crediton was not to his liking.[13] England was unusual in having cathedrals which were sited in the countryside in small settlements, Lichfield, Sherborne and Wells being other examples. European tradition, on the other hand, dictated that bishops and cathedrals should be based in towns, and Leofric, who had been educated in Europe, evidently regarded Exeter, a walled Roman city, as a more suitable place for his capital than Crediton. Later in the century like-minded bishops were to move from Lichfield to Chester, from Sherborne to Old Sarum and from Wells to Bath. The clergy at Crediton were probably also deficient in Leofric's eyes: a lax body of men (some of whom may even have been married) who lived in separate houses. He wanted clergy who would live a disciplined communal life, and it must have seemed easier to start afresh in Exeter than to change matters at Crediton. The Exeter minster offered an attractive alternative site. It was not in a flourishing state, and therefore in no position to resist the bishop's advances. Since the troubles of the early eleventh century it had failed to hold on to its property and had lost, according to Leofric, all but one of the twenty-six estates which Athelstan had given it. It had only five books, seven bells and one mass vestment, all in a fragile condition.[14] At the same time it had a usable building, a site with plenty of room for development and a relic collection which was probably unrivalled in the region. Accordingly, Leofric took over the minster's buildings and property; what he did with its clergy is not known. Next he approached the pope, Leo IX, and the king, Edward the Confessor, and obtained their permission to move his seat to Exeter. Finally, in 1050, he was enthroned as bishop in the minster, and Edward came in person with his queen to witness and approve the change.

The first cathedral, then, in Exeter was the Saxon building of a rather impoverished minster. Leofric does not seem to have organized any significant rebuilding; he was probably fully engaged in setting up his new reformed body of clergy, recovering the lost lands of the abbey and providing a proper supply of books, ornaments, vestments and bells for services. His successor, Osbern (1072–1103), the first Norman bishop, might have been expected to plan a new building, but he was a man of simple tastes and did nothing. After his death the bishopric was vacant for four years. So it was not until the reign of William Warelwast, the third bishop of Exeter (1107–1137), that the task was finally taken in hand. According to the best source, the annals of Tavistock Abbey, the building began to be constructed in 1114 and was advanced enough by 1133 for the clergy to move from the old cathedral into the new one, further eastwards.[15] This probably means that the eastern half was ready, including the choir, and that services could be held there while the western half, the nave, was completed. The nave was finished later in the twelfth century, but we do not know when. The whole building was in the Romanesque or Norman style of architecture, and its external dimensions can be worked out, more or less, from its remains.[16] It was shorter than the present cathedral, occupying the whole of the modern nave and crossing but only the two western bays of the present choir. The east end terminated in a semi-circular apse, possibly surrounded by an ambulatory. Astride the cathedral were the two great towers which survive today, linked to the interior by small openings. Little is known of the interior plan, and reconstructions are based on a few late documentary references and on comparisons with other twelfth-century churches. The choir is thought to have extended further westwards than it does now, into the first bay of the present nave. It held the high (or chief) altar, the stalls of the clergy, and the tombs of some of the bishops. Beside it were aisles, allowing processions to be made. The nave and the two side-towers contained some seven smaller altars dedicated to St Mary, St John the Baptist and other saints. Finally, in the thirteenth century, an 'administrative block' was added to the south, consisting of a chapter house for clergy meetings with an upper storey called the 'exchequer'. Here money, documents and books were kept, and the financial staff of the cathedral did their work.

The Norman church was unquestionably of cathedral proportions and, to judge from its towers, an impressive structure. It lasted, however, for only about a hundred years, and by the 1270s was already being demolished to make room for the present building in the Decorated style. Why was a new cathedral wanted? The people responsible for the change did not bother to leave us an explanation. The Exeter clergy may have looked enviously at the new Gothic buildings of their neighbours at Salisbury and Wells, or the Norman cathedral may have been unsound, requiring major rebuilding. We can point with more certainty to various practical motives for constructing a new cathedral. Since the Norman building had been planned, the clergy

THE NORMAN CATHEDRAL
(Conjectural Plan)

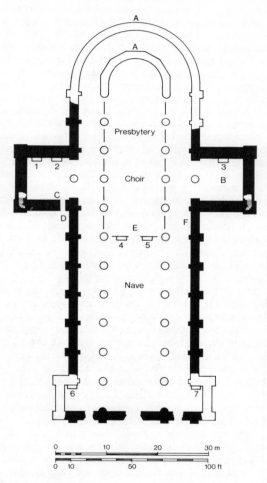

0   10   20   30 m

0   10   50   100 ft

A   Possible forms of east end

B   Possible site of Lady Chapel

C   Small door in north tower

D   Canons' bread-house

E   Approximate site of pulpitum (choir-screen)

F   "Briwere door" 13th Century

Altars

1   Cross

2   St. Paul

3   ? Lady Chapel, later St. John Baptist

4   St. Mary (nave)

5   St. John Baptist, later St. Nicholas

6   St. Edmund

7   ? St. Richard & St. Radegund

The Norman Cathedral

hád grown in numbers and importance.[17] The original twenty-four canons leading a fairly simple life had developed into a wealthy, privileged body of men, headed by a dean and other dignitaries, who probably wanted more dignified surroundings. The canons had ceased to perform most cathedral services and had recruited a large body of minor clergy to do the work instead: twenty-four vicars, twelve secondary clerks and fourteen choristers. From the 1220s a group of chantry priests began to appear, eventually totalling twenty-one. The Norman cathedral was probably not big enough for so many people. Its choir was smaller than the modern one and may have lacked space at the east end, where the clergy gathered in front of the high altar, or at the west, where they stood to sing the services. Even the aisles beside the choir may have been unsuitable for grand processions. A new, larger church could accommodate all these things and its design could also provide for developments in worship currently taking place in England. The thirteenth century saw the growing popularity of the Virgin Mary and the introduction of special services in her honour. Bishop Briwere played an important part in this respect at Exeter. In 1236 he established daily services in praise of the Virgin, to be said by five vicars, five secondaries and four choristers, and mentioned for the first time a Lady chapel where this was to be done.[18] We are not told where the chapel was – the south tower is one possibility – [19] but the accommodation, wherever situated, was probably not purpose-built and may have seemed unsatisfactory. The need for a proper Lady chapel may have been the catalyst for the remodelling of the whole cathedral, for the chapel was the first part of the new building to be constructed.

The central part of the daily worship of Our Lady was the celebration of mass in her honour. This reflected another development of the thirteenth century: the increased importance of the mass in church worship generally. It had become accepted doctrine that the bread and wine consecrated in the mass was transubstantiated, totally converted into the physical body and blood of Christ, and this 'real presence' of Christ was considered to be of great benefit to those who celebrated mass, attended it or were prayed for during the service. More and more masses were said in churches and extra altars were built to accommodate them. Lay people came to these masses to worship and wealthy people paid for masses to be celebrated for their souls when they died. The seven side-altars of the Norman cathedral were evidently too few for all the masses that needed to be said, and the provision of another six was an early priority when work began on the new cathedral.[20] It is a paradox that, as more masses were celebrated, they were regarded as more sacred. Once people believed that Christ was physically present at mass, they felt he needed a grander setting, shielded from direct contact with the public. By the late thirteenth century the altars in the Norman nave and towers were probably felt to be too simple and exposed. Accordingly, special secluded side-chapels were planned to house them in the new cathedral. The six new altars all had chapels of this kind, and very significantly the existing altars in the north and south towers were withdrawn into new chapels constructed on the east sides of the towers.[21] The altars left in the nave were eventually fenced off with screens of stone, wood or metal, one of which can still be seen: the screen of the chapel of the

16

Holy Cross (or Sylke chantry). So trends in worship were undoubtedly a powerful factor in the decision to build a new cathedral.

Thanks to the Exeter Cathedral fabric rolls, we know far more about the construction of the present cathedral than about that of its predecessor (more, indeed, than is known about the building of most English cathedrals). The rolls document all the work carried out on the building between 1279 and 1514, with various gaps.[22] As late-thirteenth and fourteenth-century records they are unparalleled even in Europe. In later times the credit for beginning the present cathedral was given to Bishop Quinil (1280–1291). Thus the 'guide-book' or 'table' displayed in the choir stated that in 1288 'the new church was founded by ... Peter Quinil'.[23] The fabric rolls, however, make it plain that the building was already well advanced in 1279, before Quinil became bishop and during the reign of his predecessor, Bishop Branscombe (1258–1280).[24] It is Branscombe, therefore, who deserves the credit for presiding over the plan for the rebuilding, although in the absence of records we do not know exactly what was due to him, to the cathedral clergy, or to the master masons who advised them. The building of the present cathedral probably started in the 1270s and went on, more or less continuously, until the early 1340s. It was effectively finished before the onset of the Black Death in 1348–9.

The work began at the east end and proceeded westwards. During the first phase, from the 1270s to 1287, the east end of the Norman building was demolished. The new Lady chapel was constructed well to the east of it, and the outer walls of the choir-aisles were raised, with chapels opening off them. The second phase, from 1288 to 1310, saw the building of the choir itself, the pillars dividing it from the choir-aisles, the upper windows and the vaulting. In the final phase, from 1310 to 1342, the choir was completed, with the high altar and screens at each end, and the Norman nave was provided with new windows, new pillars and a new vault. The west front with its stone images, originally painted in colours, was finished in about 1342. Meanwhile, the clergy had to go on holding the daily services as best they could. It is usually supposed that they moved out of the Norman choir in the 1270s and said their services in the nave, which was shut off from the unfinished choir by a temporary barrier. In 1310, when the new choir was fit to be used, they would have moved back into it to allow the nave to be finished. The new high altar was dedicated, as the previous one had been, before the completion of the whole cathedral, the dedication taking place on 18 December 1328.[25]

The money for the building came from three sources: the bishop, the cathedral authorities (dean and chapter) and the individual clergy and laity of the diocese.[26] The bishops made the largest contributions, fittingly because the cathedral (as we shall see) was their personal church and they were also the wealthiest men in the region. We do not know how much Branscombe gave and have only the vague impression that Quinil gave generously during his life and in his will. Details first emerge in the time of Quinil's successor, Thomas Bitton (1292–1307), when it is clear that the bishop, dean and chapter agreed together to contribute money regularly each year. This was perhaps in 1298. The dean and chapter undertook to pay £62. 9s. 4d., made up by a levy on each of their stipends, and the bishop promised to match this sum with twice as much, £124. 18s. 8d., making a total of £187. 8s. This enabled the rebuilding to be planned for years ahead in the knowledge that this money at least would always be available. The arrangement continued under the next bishop, Walter Stapledon (1308 – 1326), until 1325, when Stapledon, who was the king's treasurer and a very rich man, increased his share to 1000 marks (£666. 13s. 4d.) – nearly five times the previous figure. Whether this would have been a permanent increase is not known, for in the following year he was murdered in London and the next two bishops, James Berkeley (1327) and John Grandisson (1328 – 1369) were not such wealthy men. The dean and chapter went on paying their £62. 9s. 4d. until 1348 or shortly afterwards, but the bishop stopped his contribution and, in Grandisson's case, made smaller gifts of money less regularly. He continued to take an interest in the building, however, and gave it help in other ways, including gifts of timber from his estates for the woodwork needed in the construction.

The rest of the money came from the cathedral clergy individually, from the other clergy in the diocese and from the laity. Just once, in 1312, there was a tax on the clergy, sanctioned by Stapledon. It produced £90. Virtually all the money provided by individuals, however, was given voluntarily. Visitors to the cathedral put their contributions into two collection boxes, one by the statue of St Peter (called 'Old Peter') in the nave near the choir-screen and another, called the Red Chest, whose whereabouts is not clear.[27] All cathedral offerings on certain days of the year, particularly Corpus Christi and Lammas Day, seem also to have gone to the fabric. Several people left money in their wills, including one large donation of £66. 13s. 4d by the Earl of Devon in 1340, and many smaller ones of a few shillings or even pence. At first these lay contributions were not organized, but in 1324 the bishop and the cathedral authorities began a deliberate policy of encouraging them by means of indulgences.

Indulgences have come to be regarded, by Protestants especially, as one of the most corrupt and sinister institutions of the medieval Church. As practised by the cathedral and indeed by many other bodies, they seem eminently rational and respectable ways of raising money. Only the pope or a bishop could proclaim an indulgence. A bishop's indulgence offered forty days' remission of penance to anyone who carried out a specified good work – in this case the contribution of money to the cathedral fabric. The cathedral clergy had copies of the indulgence made by hand, from 400 to 800 copies every year, and these were sent to all the parish churches in the diocese, as well as to meetings of the clergy in the archdeaconries and rural deaneries. In due course the parish clergy read out the indulgence to their parishioners, and anyone who wished to contribute gave their money or valuables to the indulgence-collectors. No specific contribution was asked for, because the indulgence was meant to be available to rich and poor alike. When the givers next went to confession, they reported how much they had given. Their confessor had to make sure that they were sorry for their sins and had made an adequate contribution in relation to their means; if so, but only then, he deducted the forty days from their penance. People in the Middle Ages are often accused of 'buying' indulgences. More accurately, they donated money as we do to good causes. Like charity appeals today

18

indulgences were a sensible way of channelling money from people in general to a specific good work in one place. The proceeds from indulgences brought the cathedral over £25 a year from 1324 onwards, and it would not have been rebuilt so quickly or to such a high standard without them.

The fabric rolls not only show how the money for the rebuilding was collected but how it was spent, and thereby illustrate the process by which the cathedral was built. The expenses of the work can be divided into two main categories: men and materials. Two men were in charge of the rebuilding: the warden or clerk of the works and the master mason. The warden was one of the lesser cathedral clergy and his job was that of financier; he handled the receipts of money for the building and paid the expenses. The fabric rolls, drawn up at Michaelmas each year, were his account of these transactions. The master mason was in overall charge of the building operations, both as architect and head of the work-force. Three successive master masons are recorded in the building period: Roger the Mason (1300–1310), William Luve (1310–1313) and Thomas of Witney (1316 – 1342). Each received an annual salary of £6, later £6.13s. 4d., and a free house. Both the first two were probably Exeter men and are not recorded as working elsewhere, but Witney was a well-known architect and supervised or advised on buildings at Oxford, Wells and Winchester as well as Exeter. When the master mason was away, another senior mason took charge.

The work-force was a constantly changing one, both in numbers and trades. At one time or another it included masons, carpenters, sawyers, glaziers, smiths, roofers, plumbers, painters, carvers, plasterers, turners, goldsmiths, pavers and carters. Masons, carpenters and carters were employed for most of the time, but some of the other tradesmen were needed only for limited periods, like plumbers (for roofing work) and goldsmiths (for painting images). The fabric rolls list the names of these men and their wages in great detail, week by week. Usually about thirty different people were employed in the course of the year, and from thirteen to twenty-three in any one week. All were paid by the week, and given accommodation when necessary. Wages varied according to the status and seniority of the workers and the time of year, the hours of work being longer in summer than winter. In the early fourteenth century they ranged from 1s. 3d. to 1s. 10 ½ d. a week in winter, and from 1s. 6d. to 2s. 3d. in summer. Holidays were generous: a week each at Christmas, Easter and Whitsun, plus odd saints' days during the year; they were unpaid, however. The workmen were expected to provide their own tools, but the cathedral bore the cost of sharpening them and, in the carpenters' case, supplied protective gloves for handling rough timber.

Materials for the rebuilding were extremely diverse and came from many different sources. For stone the builders made use of thirteen quarries, of which the three most important were Beer, Branscombe and Salcombe Regis, all on cathedral property in East Devon. The stone was brought along the coast in boats and barges, unloaded near Topsham and carried the rest of the way on carts and pack-horses. Other stone was purchased from further away for special purposes, notably Purbeck 'marble' (dark limestone) from Dorset which was used in the pillars of the nave and choir, and Caen stone from Normandy, for the high altar and certain ornamental

features. Timber was also needed: alder and poplar wood for scaffolding
poles and 'Irish boards' (exactly what these were is not known) for making
'moulds' or templates to guide the stone-cutters. Oak was used for the
great beams which hold up the roof above the stone vaulting, and for timber
furnishings inside the cathedral, such as the bishop's throne. Oaks grew on
the estates belonging to the cathedral, particularly at Norton in Newton St
Cyres, and others were supplied by Bishop Grandisson from Chudleigh.
The throne, constructed in 1312, used timber from both sources and the
fabric rolls mention the immersion of the wood in the mill-pond at Norton to
season it. Iron was used for all kinds of purposes: nails and bolts for wood,
hinges, handles and locks for doors, and bars for windows. Much of this was
obtained at the great iron fair which took place every year at Lopen, near
Crewkerne in Somerset, to which the warden of the work rode off with men
and pack-horses and bought supplies for the year ahead. Lead was needed
for covering the roofs, for filling purposes and for water-pipes. Some of this
came from as far away as Boston in Lincolnshire and was transported
round the coast. Glass, both plain and coloured, had to be purchased for
glazing windows, and gold foil, silver foil and coloured paint for the
decoration of statues and carvings. The workshops, stores and workmen's
lodgings were situated in Kalendarhay behind the deanery. Here stone and
wood were piled, carts were kept and hay was stacked for the horses that
drew them. The horses were probably stabled in the same area.

With the completion of the west front in the early 1340s, work slackened
off, though it continued into the early fifteenth century with the addition of
a complete four-sided cloister on the site of the present cloister garth
together with a new chapter house and a library in the same area. After
this, a small work-force continued to be needed for maintenance, and the
fabric rolls went on being drawn up every year to record the process.

The new building has now lasted for so long – over 600 years – that it
seems the final, predestined, unalterable form for the cathedral. In fact, if
the cathedral clergy had become more wealthy and numerous, another
cathedral would have been required. Equally, if they had become fewer and
poorer, the building could not have been maintained. Its long survival is
really a testimony to the lack of violent changes in the cathedral's history,
for better or for worse. The building of c. 1270–1342 coincided with a peak
in the cathedral's prosperity. In 1348–9 the Black Death led to a slight
drop in the number of clergy, and never again were there as many on the
cathedral staff. This meant that the building remained large enough for the
clergy, and only trifling additions were made down to the Reformation. The
Reformation caused a larger fall in the number and prosperity of the clergy
and might have been catastrophic for the cathedral, as it was for the
abbeys. As we shall see, some parts of the building were disused or changed
in use after 1548, and for a very short period in the 1650s the cathedral was
radically altered and turned into two churches.[28] With this exception,
however, enough clergy, enough wealth and enough conservatism survived
the Reformation to keep the cathedral going. And since the Romantic
Movement, popular sentiment has come to the defence of the building as
well. It is now unthinkable that it could be replaced. The third cathedral
stands, and a fourth there may not be.

3

The Inside

It is easy to assume that, since the cathedral is medieval, it looked the same in the Middle Ages as it does today. This is not the case, however, either for the inside or the outside. Outside, the treasurer's house came up to the walls on the north, the conduit and the charnel-house stood close by the west of the cathedral and there was a four-sided cloister to the south, all of which made the building look less isolated, more hemmed in. To compensate for this, there were spires on both towers (until the sixteenth century) and the statues on the west front were richly painted, so the outside, although not as it is today, was still grand. The interior was different, too. The shell – walls, pillars and carvings – was the same, but the medieval fittings and furnishings have nearly all disappeared. In consequence, the character of the interior has greatly changed. Fortunately, in our imagination we can repair the losses to some extent. In the cathedral archives many stray facts about the appearance of the interior are recorded and these can be pieced together to make a composite picture. It is possible to transport ourselves back to the past and see the inside as it would have looked in the fourteenth and fifteenth centuries.

Let us begin by making our way into the building as if we were medieval visitors. Gaining entry is not difficult, because the cathedral, when it was built, was provided with six public entrances. All of them led into the nave: three on the west side, two on the south and one on the north. They still exist today, though they are not all used, and the only public entrance that has been added is the way from the south transept into the chapter house which was opened in the nineteenth century. Then, as now, the chief entrance was the middle of the three doors in the west front. Important people – bishops, kings and noblemen – entered the Close through the Broad Gate and were received in state at the great west door. The canons also used this door, at least once every day, because beside it on the north side, in the thickness of the wall, was a bread-house. Here a clerk handed out the daily allowance of loaves to each of the resident canons, the house being sited here because most of the canons went in this way, presumably.[1] The north door was used by the clergy who lived on the north-east side of the close, including some canons, perhaps, when they were not collecting their bread. The two south doors – the 'Briwere Door' at the south-east corner of the nave and the corresponding door at the south-west corner –

led into the cloisters, from which you could pass into the Close outside, or vice versa. Processions of the clergy sometimes left the cathedral via these southerly doors, and the Exeter laity liked to use them as a short cut into the building. In the 1440s the mayor and citizens said that the cloister was a 'common way' for people to enter the cathedral, but the dean and chapter, as we have seen, complained that interlopers came in from outside and played rough games in the cloister, causing damage. The chapter accordingly closed the entrance from the Close into the cloisters and thereby into the cathedral and the laity were restricted to using the doors on the west and north.[2]

Nations take care of their boundaries, and the power of a government is usually strongest at its capital and on its frontiers. So it was with the cathedral: the principal points of entry were defended and patrolled by guardians both human and superhuman. Beside the great west door stood the chapel of Bishop Grandisson and in the chapel lay the bishop in his tomb like a sentry on duty, watching the western approaches. Grandisson was a formidable bishop when alive and it was characteristic of him to choose to guard his church in death as well as in life. From 1403 onwards, a chantry priest said mass in the Grandisson chapel each day, creating the

KEY TO THE PLAN
Altars and Chapels

1.	Lady chapel	13.	St Paul
2.	St John the Evangelist	14.	St John the Baptist
3.	St Gabriel	15.	Holy Cross
4.	St George	16.	St Mary in the nave
5.	St Saviour	17.	St Nicholas
6.	High altar (Our Lady,	18.	St Michael and the tomb
	St Peter and St Paul)		of Bishop John
7.	St Thomas Becket and St Alphege	19.	Holy Ghost
8.	St Stephen and St Lawrence	20.	Trinity (Brantingham chantry)
9.	St Andrew	21.	Courtenay chantry
10.	St Katherine	22.	St Edmund the King
11.	St Mary Magdalene	23.	Grandisson chantry (? St Radegund)
12.	St James		

Images and other Features

A.	St Peter (image)	I.	Choir screen *(pulpitum)*
B.	St Paul and Our Lady (images)		with cross above
C.	Tomb of Bishop Lacy	J.	St Mary (image)
D.	Tomb of Bishop Berkeley	K.	St Michael (image)
E.	St Mary Magdalene (image)	L.	St Mary (image)
F.	Bishop's throne	M.	Font (in this area)
G.	Choir-stalls	N.	Possible site of bread-house
H.	Old Peter (image)		

Collecting Boxes

These were sited by 10, 15, 18, 20, 21, 23, A, B, C, D, H, J, L, and perhaps in other places.

EXETER CATHEDRAL, c.1270-1550

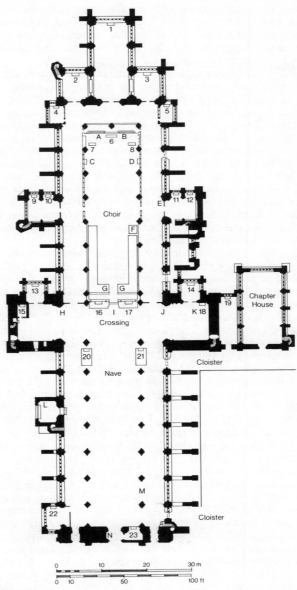

The Decorated Cathedral

body of Christ from bread and wine and thereby causing Christ himself to sanctify the entrance.[3] The north door was protected by Our Lady. Her statue stood in the porch, with a collecting box for donations,[4] and over the porch was a chamber where it is probable that the sacristans or 'custors' slept each night, ready to defend the cathedral at any time.[5] In short, the doors were important and the clergy regularly visited them on patrols, to show the flag, as it were.

On Ash Wednesday, penitent sinners were symbolically expelled from the west door, and reconciled again on Maundy Thursday. On Palm Sunday and Rogation days, processions of clergy passed through the doors, along the Close and round the city streets.[6] Eventually, the custom grew up that the choristers should visit the principal doors daily, singing antiphons and saying prayers. In 1436 Chancellor Orum bequeathed the choristers £40 to sing an antiphon each day over his grave in the north porch (the antiphon was probably in honour of the Virgin Mary, whose statue stood there)[7] and in 1532 we hear of the choristers going out of the west doors to sing an antiphon in the charnel chapel near by before returning to the doors to recite the De Profundis.[8] The worship of the church, therefore, pulsed regularly from its heart in the choir to its extremities at the doors, and the edges of the building were patrolled and kept holy like the edges of the Close and the cemetery outside.

On entering the cathedral by the great west door, the visitor saw, as we still do, the best view of the inside of the building: a perfect combination of dimension and design. The architecture was all of a piece, in the same harmonious Decorated style. Vertically, the eye took in the columns of the nave, marching in two straight lines towards the choir-screen and throwing out curved ribs that met at the centre of the vault. The effect was that of a great avenue of trees. The floor of the cathedral, free of chairs, looked wider and more spacious than it does today, and the great length of the building was suggested by the central line of the vaulting, speeding off towards the great east window in the distance. Yet not all was revealed, for the choir was hidden by the screen. This gave an air of mystery and 'more to come'. The grandeur of the proportions was enhanced by the profusion of ornament and colour: painted corbels and bosses, and coats of arms in the stained glass of the windows. The visitor saw a great church, but more than this he saw an image of the Church itself. Above him, on the walls, the roof and the windows, was the Church Triumphant: carved and painted saints and angels. Before him, on his own level, was the Church Militant: his fellow men and women, some at prayer and others gossiping or doing business deals. And underneath his feet was the Church Dormant: the dead awaiting the sound of the final trumpet. The floor of the cathedral was a great covered burial-ground, paved with the gravestones of canons and superior citizens, who were privileged to await the trumpet in the dry, unlike the common people buried in the damp untidy cemetery outside.

As soon as the visitor had finished admiring the view, he would observe that the west end of the nave where he stood was relatively empty, with little in the way of fittings. On the south side, near where it stands today, was the font containing the holy water needed for services and sometimes used for christening babies.[9] These were presumably the babies of

24

important people, dipped as a special favour, for no children were born inside the cathedral precincts until after the Reformation, when the clergy were allowed to marry. In the north-west corner was the chapel of St Edmund. A chantry priest said mass here each day from 1292 until the Black Death for the soul of the murdered precentor, who had died not far outside the cathedral doors. When the Black Death caused a shortage of clergy, these masses were apparently discontinued and St Edmund's chapel fell into disuse.[10] It is not mentioned as such after 1337, and the likelihood is that is was altered for other purposes. By the eighteenth century, and possibly much earlier, it was the meeting-place of the bishop's Consistory Court.[11]

After 1350, therefore, any visitor to the cathedral entered a nave whose west end did not count very much in religious terms, except when processions passed through. As he proceeded eastwards, however, the spiritual atmosphere of the building gradually increased. There was little or none in the first four bays, except for the carvings and stained glass, but high up on the left-hand side of the fifth bay he would have seen the minstrels' gallery, which may have been intended to hold a choir at times of great processions up the nave, at the entrance of a bishop or a king, for example. There are two niches below the minstrels' gallery which are empty today but probably once held little statues of the Virgin and St Peter, the chief patron saints of the cathedral.[12] The sixth bay from the west was more important still. From the end of the fourteenth century it contained two chapels: one on each side, between the pillars of the nave arcades. Each chapel was surrounded by screens of wood or stone, and must have looked rather like the chapels found in the same position in Wells Cathedral. The chapel on the north side housed the tomb-slab of Bishop Brantingham, and that on the south side the altar tomb of the Earl and Countess of Devon. Daily masses were celebrated by chantry priests at both these chapels.[13] Lay people attended them and gave offerings, for the chapels each had collecting boxes. This part of the nave was therefore in regular use for worship.[14]

The rest of the nave, from the two chapels eastwards towards the choir-screen, was probably the forum for the cathedral sermons. From 1337, if not earlier, sermons were regularly preached during Advent and Lent, as well as on some of the great festivals, by the canons, by local Franciscan and Dominican friars, or by visiting Oxford scholars.[15] We do not know exactly where they stood to preach, because although there are several references to the 'pulpitum' and the 'pulpit', these words normally meant the choir-screen; we cannot be sure if or when they came to signify the modern, separate, kind of pulpit. It may well be that until the Reformation preachers held forth from the top of the screen, and that a pulpit proper was only installed after that date. At any rate, it seems very likely that people assembled for sermons in this part of the church, the unimportant ones standing or squatting, and the important ones sitting on moveable seats. In 1510 the custors were paid fourpence for providing a bench for the mayor and his colleagues to rest on at sermon-time; other wealthy people may have brought their own.[16]

The area between the end of the nave and the choir-screen is known as the 'crossing'. It is a wide space, spreading northwards and southwards into the transepts, and was important for worship as well as preaching. Here the visitor encountered a series of images that formed the visual and religious climax of his progress up the nave. Above the screen stood the great cross, richly painted in gold, silver and other colours, with lights burning in front of it.[17] Below, at ground level, was a row of chapels and statues reminiscent of an iconostasis or image-screen in an Orthodox church.[18] Counting from left to right, there were as follows: 1. In the north-east corner, the altar of the Holy Cross, perhaps with a cross on the wall above to indicate the fact. The altar was closed off by a screen, the present version of which was built by Precentor Sylke in about 1500. 2. The chapel of St Paul. 3. Between the chapel and the entrance to the north choir-aisle, the large statue called 'Old Peter'. 4. The choir-screen, solid (not pierced with windows as it is today) except for one central doorway. On each side of the doorway, protected by screens, there was an altar: the altar of St Mary on the left and that of St Nicholas on the right. 5. A large statue of the Virgin to the right of the south choir-aisle, corresponding to Old Peter. 6. The chapel of St John the Baptist. 7. In the right-hand corner, the tomb of Bishop John the Chanter (d. 1191). 8. At the end of the fourteenth century, an image of St Michael was also put in the right-hand corner. It is first mentioned in 1398, when Canon John Michel was buried in front of it, and he may well have been responsible for installing it. Shortly afterwards, an altar was placed in front of the statue to balance the Cross altar in the opposite corner. This altar of St Michael was moveable, not fixed, and does not appear to have been screened off like the other altars.[19]

The line of images was an important focus of worship in the cathedral. Processions generally entered the choir by the entrance in the centre of the screen and paused to make a station there in honour of the high cross. In 1514 Bishop Oldham instituted the singing of a daily antiphon by the choir, also in the cross's honour.[20] During the later Middle Ages, at least one mass was said every day at the altars of the Holy Cross, St Paul, St Mary, St Nicholas and St John the Baptist, and also, by 1530, at the altar of St Michael.[21] The most important masses were those which were said at the altar of St Mary. It was generally known as the 'Bratton' or 'Barton' altar because the chantry priests who ministered there prayed for the soul of Henry de Bracton (i.e. 'of Bratton'), the famous lawyer and cathedral chancellor who was buried near by. The Bratton masses were the first masses of the day, celebrated at dawn, and no other mass could be said until they were over.[22] They corresponded to what in other towns were often called 'morrow masses', and were popular with pious citizens who got up early to attend mass before work.

Lay people, therefore, came to the cathedral at daybreak, and probably at other hours of the day, to hear the masses, or to listen to the choral services taking place beyond the choir-screen. In the services for Holy Innocents' Day, for example, we are told that the chorister who acted as 'boy bishop' walked to the screen and blessed the people who were gathered there.[23] The clergy were not slow to exploit the piety of the laity who frequented this area. Several collection boxes were provided for their offerings: one in the north tower by the Cross altar, one by the statue of St Peter, another by that of the Virgin, and one in the south tower by the tomb of Bishop John (this box was later transferred to the statue of St Michael).[24] The statue of St Peter deserves a few words to itself. It was said to have once stood by the high altar at the east end of the choir and to have been removed in the 1320s when Bishop Stapledon remodelled the high altar.[25] The statue may well have stood there, but it was much older than Stapledon, for it is mentioned as early as 1286. Sums of between £2 and £4 a year were collected in the box beside it, which was specially designated for contributions to the fabric of the cathedral.[26]

When our visitor had thoroughly inspected the crossing and the transepts, he would wish to explore further eastwards. It is not clear whether visitors (other than clergy and noblemen) were allowed to pass into the choir by the door in the screen, but they could certainly enter the two choir-aisles and get into the eastern parts of the church by this means. In the architectural plan of the cathedral, the two choir-aisles were more or less symmetrical and equal in status. Both were routes for processions. On Sunday mornings before high mass, the clergy went out of the choir by the north entrance into the north choir-aisle, walked through the retrochoir behind the high altar and down the south choir-aisle into the nave before returning under the choir-screen. Both aisles were burial-places for canons and knights, like the nave, and there was a double chantry-chapel in each, on the side opposite the choir. In terms of the use they received, however, the two aisles were not equal and their histories were different. In the 1330s and 1340s our visitor would probably have entered the south choir-aisle in the first instance. This was because Bishop Berkeley, who was buried between the choir and the south aisle in 1327, was venerated as a saint, and local people came to pray, give money and light candles at his tomb. The cult of Bishop Berkeley was very popular until the mid-1340s, after which it dwindled away, dying out altogether in about the 1370s.[27] Not long afterwards, the south choir-aisle lost its chantry-chapel, dedicated to St Mary Magdalene and St James. This chapel was in full use in the late thirteenth century and at least one and perhaps two chantry priests were attached to it until the Black Death. After the Black Death, the chantry-chapel, like that of St Edmund, appears to have lost its priests and it was converted for a more menial function: a vestry for the cathedral clergy. In 1425 the altars were still in the chapel, but their dedications had begun to be forgotten and they were simply referred to as 'the altars in the vestry'; by 1506 they had disappeared altogether.[28] By the middle of the fifteenth century, all that remained of their original worship was a statue of St Mary Magdalene in the south choir-aisle just outside the chapel entrance.[29]

The north choir-aisle, on the other hand, tended to grow in importance as the south aisle waned. It too had a double chapel, dedicated to St Andrew and St Katherine, and it also housed the exchequer. This had been moved to the room above the chapel in about the 1280s from its previous site above the chapter house. The exchequer was the cathedral's financial centre and was staffed by two of the canons acting as stewards, with the assistance of two clerks selected from the lesser clergy.[30] They kept the cathedral accounts and records and made small payments to the clergy throughout the year, for attending special services and so on. The rest of the clergy

must often have climbed the stairs to the exchequer to collect their money
so often that in 1454 one canon asked to be buried not 'outside the chapel of
St Katherine' but 'by the way to the exchequer'.[31] Unlike the chapel in the
south choir-aisle, the one in the north choir-aisle remained in use after the
Black Death and went on being served by priests. The altar of St Katherine
was particularly popular with the Exeter laity; it had a collection box
which shows that offerings were made there, and by 1521 the Mayor of
Exeter himself was accustomed to visit the altar and to hear mass said
there by his own chaplain.[32] Increasingly, therefore, in the late fourteenth
and early fifteenth centuries, our visitor would have been more likely to
enter the north choir-aisle than the south, and he would certainly have done
so after 1455, when Bishop Lacy died. Lacy repeated the success of
Berkeley in inspiring a saint-cult, and by the 1460s pilgrims were assemb
ling to pray at his tomb in the north choir-aisle, just as they had previously
done at Berkeley's.[33] The growing popularity of the north aisle is confirmed
by the fact that in the fifteenth century more canons chose to be buried
there than in the south aisle.

Whichever of the aisles our visitor entered, he would eventually find
himself in the retrochoir, behind the high altar. This was another important
part of the church, and one whose status did not diminish with time. Its
focus was the Lady chapel, where three daily services were said in honour of
the Virgin. It seems that these services attracted lay worshippers. An
indulgence was granted in 1324 to people who attended mass in the Lady
chapel,[34] and by 1506 some of the major cathedral relics were kept and
could presumably be viewed there, including bones belonging to St Mary
Magdalene and part of the head of St Nicasius of Rheims.[35] Daily masses
were said in all of the little chapels beside the Lady chapel: those of St John
the Evangelist on the north side and St Gabriel on the south, and the two
chapels of St George and St Saviour, which were added in the early sixteenth century.[36] The east end of the cathedral was a coveted place of
burial. At least five bishops chose to lie there: Quinil in the centre of the
Lady chapel, Branscombe and Stafford at its corners, and Oldham in the
chapel of St Saviour. Several of the canons were entombed in these chapels
or in the floor of the retrochoir outside.

We have brought our visitor to the choir last of all, because it was the
most important part of the cathedral, but if he himself had been important
he might have been conducted there immediately, as one imagines the
bishop or visiting royalty being taken from the west door straight to the
choir and the high altar. Ordinary lay people were barred from the choir
during services and the choir entrances had gates that could be locked, but
a gratuity to the custors probably opened all doors, and in default of that
you could get a restricted view of the choir by peeping through the screens
from the choir-aisles. The western part of the choir was much as it is today.
It held the bishop's throne and the stalls for the clergy; the latter are
modern now, but they are laid out in a similar way to their medieval
predecessors. The eastern part or presbytery, on the other hand, was quite
different and more resplendent.[37] Across the whole of the east end stood a
wide stone screen, twenty feet high, richly carved and decorated with
niches containing images. At the top of the screen rose a forest of pinnacles,

like the pinnacles that still rise up today from the sedilia on the south side of the presbytery. The high altar was placed against the central part of the great carved screen. Behind the altar was a silver retable (a carved vertical panel), on it stood a cross and candlesticks, and in front of it was draped a beautiful embroidered frontal-cloth. Above the altar, hanging by wires from the roof, was a dove – representing the Holy Spirit – attended by flying angels, so that it looked as though the Spirit of God Himself was hovering overhead. Around the altar were large statues of the patron saints of the cathedral: Peter on the north side, Paul on the south, and the Virgin Mary close to St Paul. Collecting boxes lay at their feet.[38] The ensemble was completed by two small 'collateral' altars, which were placed at the side of the presbytery and probably well forward. The northern one was dedicated to St Thomas Becket and St Alphege, and the other to St Stephen and St Lawrence. The effect must have been striking: a blend of carved and painted stonework and images, and ornately worked embroideries and carpets all bathed in a rich and varied light from the stained-glass windows. This was the holiest part of the church, where only bishops were allowed to be buried. Six or seven were interred in the floor or round the choir walls: Marshal, Briwere, Bitton, Stapledon, Berkeley, Lacy and, possibly, Blund.

We have looked at the cathedral as a beautiful building devoted to the

Bishop Branscombe's Tomb
Bishop Walter Branscombe, 'Walter the Good' (d. 1280), began the building of the modern cathedral. His splendid tomb reminds us of this fact, and also proclaims that the cathedral is the church of the local bishop.

worship of God, but we must not forget that it was also a place of work for the clergy, where various practical tasks were carried out. There was a good deal of clutter, as there is today. Screens and gates surrounded the lesser altars to protect them from the public and some of the tombs were railed off. A profusion of books lay about, because although the cathedral acquired a library building in 1412, a good many volumes remained in the church as aids to worship.[39] Several of these were placed on, or chained to the desks in front of the choir-stalls; others were chained behind the screen of the high altar and to the inner walls of the presbytery, so that outside service times the east end of the choir must have looked like a library, with clergy looking at books. Yet more volumes were chained in the north choir aisle behind the choir-stalls; these were mainly books on canon and civil law. The cathedral had several functions besides worship; it was a library, a vestry, a muniment room (the archives were eventually housed above the south choir-aisle chapel), an exchequer and a bread pantry. Indeed, even as a place of worship, in some respects the building resembled a modern factory. Each day it turned out a dozen services of prayer, some twenty-five masses and various subsidiary observances. Like a factory, it had a clock; its bells were its factory siren, and it even had a clocking-on system: as the clergy arrived for services their names were ticked off to record their attendance. Long before the Protestant Ethic or the Industrial Revolution some of their most characteristic methods and ideas were anticipated by the churches of the Middle Ages.

4

The Clergy

The inside of a church tells us not only about religion, but about people. As well as altars and statues it contains furniture, decorations and monuments which indicate who runs the building and who uses it. The tombs of the kings in Westminster Abbey, for example, show that the abbey is a royal foundation under close royal patronage. Equally, at Tewkesbury, the lords and ladies buried around the high altar demonstrate that the church, in medieval times, was under the patronage of a great baronial family, the Despensers. No visitor to Exeter Cathedral in the Middle Ages could have been in any doubt that this was a bishop's church. Beside the choir-stalls stood the bishop's throne, its splendid spire soaring to the roof. On the choir-screens, in the glass of the windows and on many of the altar frontals and clergy vestments were bishops' coats of arms. And all around the east end of the building were their tombs: several as large as altars and some with sculptured figures, all more splendid than the plain tomb-slabs of the rest of the clergy. There was a small lay presence: the Courtenay monument in the nave, the Speke chapel and two or three effigies of knights. But these were few, and the other furnishings which nowadays make the cathedral into a sort of public mausoleum – regimental banners, war memorials and plaques to famous men – were entirely absent. The glory of the bishops shone undimmed.

Cathedrals are the bishops' churches and take their name from the word for a bishop's seat or throne: his *cathedra*.[1] Even today a bishop's term of office starts symbolically with his enthronement in the cathedral; he leads the services on great occasions, and he appoints most of the chief clergy of the establishment. In the early centuries of Church history, bishops and their cathedrals were even more closely connected. Dioceses in Mediterranean lands were often small and based on a single city. The bishop lived near the cathedral, he used it for his regular worship, and his personal staff of clergy were also the staff of the cathedral. In medieval England this relationship was weaker. English dioceses were larger than they are today, and English bishops were more important politically.

Until 1877 the diocese of Exeter covered the whole of Devon and Cornwall, and the bishop owned estates widely scattered over both counties. He constantly travelled about, visiting his properties, seeing to the affairs of the diocese and going to London to attend Parliament and Church councils. He had a palace at Exeter (as the Bishop of Exeter has today) but was rarely there. Instead he moved around a number of houses in different parts of the country, in exactly the same way as the king and the great nobility.[2] When he was in London he lived at Exeter House in the Strand. When he was travelling to and from the capital, he stayed at his houses at West Horsley in Surrey and Farringdon in Hampshire, or at Chidham in Sussex, near Bosham, where he also had property. In Devon he had several manor-houses in the countryside, and lived in them rather than in Exeter, particularly at Bishop's Court (north of Clyst St Mary), Bishopsteignton, Chudleigh and Paignton. He was, indeed, the first to discover the delights of the 'English Riviera'. This travelling made it impossible for the same band of clergy to accompany the bishop and staff the cathedral. Accordingly, they split into two groups. The smaller one, the bishop's household staff, went with him, helped him to administer the diocese and held services for him in the chapel of whichever house he was living in. The larger group settled down permanently in Exeter, and ran the services and affairs of the cathedral.

The bishop, then, was rarely seen in his principal church. Once he had been enthroned at the beginning of his reign, he merely visited a few times a year. Even his ordinations of clergy were often held in other convenient churches or chapels where he was staying. Despite these absences, however, he continued to possess a good many rights and powers in the cathedral. He could attend the services, sitting on his throne, and any cleric who entered the choir by the north or south entrances had to bow to him. If he was present at one of the great festivals he could lead the service of matins or celebrate the chief mass of the day.[3] He had the power of patronage, since he appointed all the major members of the cathedral staff except for the dean: the precentor, chancellor, treasurer, archdeacons and canons. He issued the fundamental laws by which the cathedral was governed. The dean and chapter ran the place on a day-to-day basis and made minor decisions, but major changes to cathedral government had to be approved by the bishop. The statutes by which the clergy were governed up to the Reformation were a miscellaneous collection of bishops' pronouncements from the twelfth century onwards.[4] The Ordinal, which stated how the services were to be carried out, was issued by Bishop Grandisson in 1337.[5] Finally, the bishop had the power to visit, in the formal sense of the word. Every few years he came to enquire into the way that the cathedral was being run, and all the clergy from the dean downwards had to appear before him and answer his questions. When the bishop had thoroughly satisfied himself about the situation, he issued orders for this or that to be changed or enforced. These orders had the status of statutes and held good in the short and in the long term.[6]

The clergy must sometimes have found the bishop's attentions irksome. Although they were 'his' clergy in a very special sense, they often owed their appointments not to him but to one of his predecessors, and they had ties of friendship with one another which did not always harmonize with their duty to the bishop. Like all of us they were inclined to modify their duties and perquisites to make their lives more comfortable, and they cannot have relished visitation time, when their improvements were exposed, denounced and forbidden. The clergy did not quarrel with the bishop, however, as seriously as they did with the city authorities. Despite his role as a disciplinarian, the bishop was a valuable friend and benefactor. He could always be relied on to assist the cathedral against the mayor, or to excommunicate wicked people who attacked cathedral personnel and property. He was a generous giver of money, goods and endowments. Although the cathedral owed some of its property to kings and wealthy laymen, the majority of its wealth had come from the bishops. They gave it land (notably Leofric's gift of the manor of Bampton in Oxfordshire) and money (such as Stapledon's contribution to the new buildings in the 1320s). They granted it parish churches, and transferred or 'appropriated' the tithes paid by the parishioners from these churches to the cathedral. They issued indulgences to encourage lay people to visit the building or to give it money. And they handed over silver and vestments for its worship, particularly when they died. 'I give and bequeath to the church of Exeter,' wrote Grandisson in his will of 1369, 'my best white vestments ... all embroidered with the rosary in gold and my arms and with demi angels ... four of my best copes ... a gilt cross having precious stones on either side ... two images of the apostles Peter and Paul of silver gilt and a golden thurible ... the silver basin belonging to my chapel ... ' and so on and so on.[7] When they died, the bishops were probably sincerely mourned at the cathedral and nearly all of them chose to be buried there. Only about four of the twenty-five who died in office between 1050 and 1554 were entombed elsewhere, one or two of these by accident.[8] Former bishops were regularly prayed for in cathedral services and most had daily or annual masses said in their honour right down to the Reformation.

There were nineteen cathedrals in medieval England, ten of them monasteries and the other nine 'secular' foundations, to use the technical term. The clergy of the monastic cathedrals, such as Canterbury, Durham and Worcester, were monks who lived communally, possessed no private property and were restricted in the extent to which they could leave the premises. Secular cathedrals, on the other hand, like St Paul's, Salisbury and York, were staffed by clergy called canons who lived separately in private houses, were allowed to own personal property and could go about the world with few restrictions. Exeter Cathedral was a secular foundation, but unlike most of the others, it also had certain monastic characteristics. When Leofric founded it in 1050, he chose to staff it with canons, not monks, probably so that they would be free to travel about and carry out tasks in the world. But he wished them to live communally, like monks, and the constitution which he gave them – the *Rule of St Chrodegang* – laid down that they should sleep like monks in a common dormitory, eat in a common refectory and live inside an enclosure guarded by a porter.[9] These arrangements did not last long after Leofric's death in 1072. During the next 200 years, the life of the canons changed to become more individual and more comfortable. By the middle of the twelfth century, they had given up living together and each canon had moved to a private house, where he slept and had his meals by himself. This was what canons did in the other secular cathedrals, and accounts for the characteristic 'village' appearance of cathedral closes compared with the institutional, integrated buildings of a monastery.

Exeter, then, was fully secular early on in the way that its clergy lived, but it kept something of its original communal nature in the way that they were paid.[10] Canons' stipends were known as their 'prebends' (supplies), a term related to the word 'provender' – hence the name 'prebendary' by which canons are sometimes called. At the other secular cathedrals each canon was given one of the estates as his prebend, the estates varying in value and consequently in income, and he got this income whether or not he lived near the cathedral and fulfilled any duties. It would seem scandalous today for cathedral canons to be paid for doing no work, but in the Middle Ages the Church had no central funds, and canonries were useful ways of paying bishops' administrators, clergy in the king's service and university scholars. Exeter was different. Its twenty-four canons were paid more equally and they got very little unless they resided locally and carried out duties. Each canon received £4 a year unconditionally, but that was not very much. The rest of the cathedral's income was shared among only the resident canons. The division was made by two canons called stewards, who did the task for a year or two in turn. They paid out daily allowances to every resident canon which consisted of money (ranging from 12d. on ordinary days to 18d. at festivals) and bread (three loaves of pure white flour, weighing 3 ⅔ lb each).[11] Any surplus income was paid out four times a year to those canons who had resided in Exeter for at least half of the previous quarter (forty-six days). This had a profound effect on the cathedral community. Whereas at the other secular cathedrals there were only a few resident canons and most lived far away, at Exeter the reverse was true. Only a handful failed to reside, and the majority – about sixteen to eighteen out of the twenty-four – kept frequent residence in their houses round the Close, taking part in the worship and government of the cathedral.

They also grew grander and wealthier than Leofric had intended. He had planned that the canons should live a relatively modest life, centred on saying the daily services at the cathedral,[12] but in the two centuries after his death they became a managerial class who supervised the saying of services by others, rather than doing so themselves. Gradually, special offices or 'dignities' began to be established.[13] By the middle of the twelfth century, in addition to the two stewards there was a precentor, responsible for the organization of the services, and a treasurer, who was in charge of the church's candles, vestments and ornaments. The four archdeacons of the Exeter diocese were also based at Exeter and came to be associated with the cathedral. In the 1220s Bishop Briwere increased the number of dignities by introducing a dean and a chancellor, and from then onwards Exeter possessed the characteristic 'four-square' leadership common to all the secular cathedrals: dean, precentor, chancellor and treasurer. Later, in 1284, an office of subdean was also created.[14] Under Briwere's arrangements the dean was the chief officer of the cathedral, acting as chairman of the canons' meetings or 'chapters' and responsible for the discipline of these and the other clergy.[15] The precentor continued to organize the cathedral services and looked after the choristers. The chancellor corrected mistakes in the (handwritten) service-books, drafted business letters, and eventually, in 1283, began giving lectures on theology or canon (Church) law to the local clergy.[16] The treasurer remained in charge of the cathedral's moveable property, and the subdean acted as confessor or 'penitentiary' to

A Cathedral Canon

Canon William Langton (d. 1414) prays to Christ for mercy. His handsome features and beautiful cope symbolize the elegance and wealth of cathedral canons, while the inscription underneath reveals his elevated social origins: he was a relative of Bishop Stafford, who appointed him.

the rest of the cathedral clergy. Briwere provided extra stipends for the dean and the precentor (the treasurer already had one), and in due course the same was done for the chancellor and subdean. The dignitaries were usually canons too, so they got the canons' allowances as well, and since the cathedral properties and revenues steadily increased from Leofric's time, by the thirteenth century even the ordinary canons were well paid. They could also supplement their income by becoming rectors or vicars of parish churches, and doing their duties there by deputy. It is difficult to summarize their financial status exactly, but they were undoubtedly wealthy men.

Most of them were born to wealth, too, rather than men who had worked their way up from nothing. In general, the Exeter canons came from the families of country gentlemen, yeomen or wealthy citizens, like the Lechlades, Lercedeknes, Shillingfords and Stapledons. Some were local men, others were brought by the bishops from elsewhere in the kingdom. There was family money behind them – many had been to university – and family influence had aided their advancement in the Church and brought them to the bishop's notice. This did not prevent them from being capable and intelligent as well, of course. A few poorer clergy were occasionally given canonries, but not often, because such people could not keep up the standard of living expected of a canon, and by the Reformation it had been laid down that no one could become a resident canon unless he could deposit £40 (a large sum) in the cathedral exchequer.[17]

The life-style of a canon had to be expansive. Even today the canons' houses in the Close look large and impressive and in the Middle Ages they were bigger than they are now, with a great hall, a chapel, private chambers, a kitchen and store-rooms.[18] To the rear lay stables and gardens with fruit-trees.[19] Indoors were sumptuous possessions and servants to look after them. The canons went to services in sober black and white, but out of church they liked to wear scarlet gowns and hoods trimmed with expensive fur to emphasize their rank.[20] Their private rooms were decorated with wall-hangings and their beds had canopies and curtains of the finest fabrics. At meals they washed their hands with silver ewers and basins, helped themselves to food with silver spoons and drank their wine from silver cups embellished with covers, mottoes, initials or lions' feet. Grandisson grumbled that some canons preferred hawking and hunting to duties in church.[21] To be fair, the majority probably did have clerical vocations of a sort, but they were gentlemen by upbringing and saw no reason why the two kinds of life should not be combined.

The basic duty of the canons was to pray. Every medieval cleric had to say eight services each day: the night service of matins and seven daytime ones. Many also celebrated mass.[22] Leofric had intended his canons to say these services together in the cathedral, but by the thirteenth century this was no longer done. The canons said their services in their own houses (or wherever they were), and had to go to the cathedral for only two: matins and one of the major daytime services (prime, high mass or vespers).[23] Even this became diluted; by 1268 the canons could miss one matins a week in order to have a quiet night, and by 1336 they could avoid matins altogether if they went to high mass in the morning and vespers in the afternoon.[24]

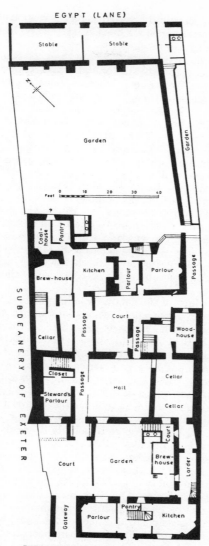

A Canon's House
Number 7, The Close, now The Devon and Exeter Institution, but originally a canon's house. This plan of 1764 shows some of its medieval features, including the great hall in the centre, kitchens, chambers, stables and a garden.

Cathedral services accordingly ceased to be the responsibility of the canons alone, except on special occasions like Christmas and Easter, and the duties passed to other clergy, as we shall see.

What did the canons do instead? They had, of course, administrative tasks. The dean, precentor, chancellor and treasurer had their specific functions and so did the two canons who acted as stewards. The dean and canons met from time to time, 'in chapter' as it was called, to run the cathedral's affairs – hence the term 'dean and chapter', denoting the cathedral's governing body. Several were also active in the administration of the diocese. Some were archdeacons, responsible for supervising the parishes, and others ran the Church courts which met in Exeter to deal with moral crimes, wills and other matters.[25] Many canons possessed books chiefly service-books and books on canon law and theology, and the cathedral library was also well stocked in these subjects. Some of the time was therefore spent in study, particularly the study of law, by those who ran Church affairs, and of theology, by those who preached sermons, as some of the canons did.[26] Their study was for practical purposes, however rather than pure research as we understand it. A few of the canons were important medieval writers – Henry Bracton the lawyer, Thomas Buckingham the theologian and Adam Murimuth the chronicler – but they wrote most of their books in London or at university, before or after the time that they lived in Exeter.[27]

The other major duty of the canons was hospitality. Each resident canon was expected to keep a household of servants and to give food and accommodation to other people. Bishops regarded this duty seriously and it figures prominently in their visitations.[28] Hospitality was due both to the other cathedral clergy and to outsiders. On coming into residence for the first time, all canons had to give a series of feasts for their fellow canons and the lesser clergy. They each spent as much as £50 in this way, according to Bishop Oldham, who ended the practice in 1511.[29] Every canon also had a deputy or 'vicar choral' who took his place at cathedral services, and a secondary clerk (similar to a choral scholar) and a chorister were often assigned to him. All these received their daily meals in his house. Then there were visitors. It is not likely that the canons provided food and lodging for every outsider who asked for it; if they had done, Exeter would not have needed inns, of which there were several. But they certainly entertained royalty, and probably also the sheriff, the king's Justices, noblemen, gentlemen and visiting clergy. The sixteenth-century cathedral statutes lay particular stress on the canons being in residence at major festivals and when the assizes and sessions of Justices of the Peace were held in Exeter.[30] It was also a universal obligation on wealthy people, clergy or laity, to give their surplus food to the poor. The canons therefore lived a public life, with many visitors frequenting their houses and beggars waiting for the scraps outside. And they were open-handed in death. From about 1200 onwards every canon was allowed to receive his bread and allowances for one year after he died, in order to augment his will, and this together with the money he had earned in life was often given to charity.[31] Canons' wills are full of bequests to poor scholars, poor clergy, the Exeter hospitals and poor people in general.

The withdrawal of the canons from most cathedral services meant that others had to be found to take their place. Like all the secular cathedrals, Exeter employed large numbers of minor clergy for this purpose.[32] There were probably boys and adolescents from the earliest days, since they are mentioned in Leofric's *Rule,* and adult clergy were assisting the canons by the middle of the twelfth century. By the early thirteenth century there were three official groups of minor clergy: fourteen boy choristers aged between about seven and fourteen, twelve adolescent secondaries aged between eighteen and twenty-four, and twenty-four vicars choral, all priests and therefore over the age of twenty-four. Their primary task was to say the daily services in the cathedral choir, and they had to say them all, except for the choristers, who spent part of the day in church and part in school. Later, in the second half of the thirteenth century, a fourth group of clergy appeared: the annuellars. This was the Exeter name for those known elsewhere as chantry priests. The annuellars were adult clergy, like the vicars choral, and there were eventually twenty-one of them. They were established privately by wealthy people who gave the cathedral property with which to pay a priest to celebrate mass once a day for ever, with prayers during the mass for the soul of the founder concerned. The dean and chapter also required the annuellars to attend the daily services like the vicars and secondaries. Many minor clergy did useful administrative tasks around the place. They provided the assistants of the precentor and the treasurer – the succentor and the subtreasurer – and a clerk and subclerk to help the stewards run the exchequer. They served as clerk of the works in charge of the cathedral stonework, clerk of the Lady chapel, and clerk of the canons' bread allowance. And they kept guard. Four of them acted as 'custors' or virgers to patrol the inside of the cathedral, a fifth as keeper of the library and a sixth as porter of the Close gates. These offices carried with them small but useful extra salaries.

The minor clergy developed, rather than being deliberately founded, and for a long time they were rather haphazardly organized. Vicars, secondaries and choristers were closely dependent on the canons; indeed, they were members of their households. Right up to the early sixteenth century they ate with their canons, not together in groups, and they had to do domestic duties such as attending their masters to and from the cathedral. Canons had to be warned against using their vicars on personal business when they were needed in church. Annuellars, being privately funded, were free of these ties, but they did not get the benefit of the meals. Accommodation arrangements varied. The secondaries and some vicars may have slept in their canons' houses, but other vicars and the annuellars rented houses in the Close from the cathedral chapter and lived there in groups.

The choristers were the first to be given a special building to live in: the choristers' house, first mentioned in 1276, stood next to the deanery, opposite the south-west corner of the nave. A century later Bishop Brantingham decided that it was undesirable for the vicars to live scattered about in private rooms without supervision. In 1387 he built a special college for them in Kalendarhay, behind the deanery.[33] The college was a double row of little houses divided into single chambers, with a common hall at the end of the street, similar to the vicars' college at Wells but not as

The College of Vicars Choral
*The college in 1889, not long before its disappearance. At the west end
stood the vicars' hall (now ruined), and on its right one of the two rows of
houses in which twenty vicars originally lived in separate chambers.*

large. The Exeter buildings, unfortunately, were gradually obliterated in the nineteenth and twentieth centuries. The vicars were reluctant to forsake their cosy lodgings for the college, but the bishop compelled them to come in, and eventually they got used to it. Early in the sixteenth century they started to have their meals there and ceased to eat with the canons. The annuellars did not acquire a common dwelling-house until 1528. This building stood somewhere south-east of St Martin's Church and was probably divided into single chambers, but it is not known if there was a kitchen or dining-room. The house, in any case, had a very brief existence, for the annuellars were abolished at the Reformation in 1548.

Minor clergy were less well-paid than canons and came from lower down the social scale, from the families of prosperous peasants (husbandmen, as they were called) or substantial craftsmen and shopkeepers. Most of them were from Devon and Cornwall. In the middle of the sixteenth century the parents of the choristers included two gentlemen (but in one case the boy was illegitimate), a merchant, two yeomen, five husbandmen, a brewer, a miller, a weaver and a widow. Some of the minor clergy had the same surname as some of the canons and were probably their junior relatives. Despite their relatively low incomes, the posts were attractive and, as always, status and influence counted in obtaining them. A chorister received free food, lodging and training and picked up fees for special services. When he was eighteen or so, he could become a secondary, which gave him up to six more years of paid work. In their turn, secondaries could count on the cathedral sponsoring them to be ordained as priests, and had a good chance of becoming annuellars and vicars choral. Adult minor clergy had their own opportunities for advancement. They could add to their everyday wages by taking on minor cathedral offices, and sometimes they were also allowed to be rectors of the small parish churches in Exeter. The cathedral held the patronage of a good many other churches in Devon and Cornwall, like Branscombe, Colyton and Salcombe Regis in East Devon, for example, and vicars and annuellars were sometimes promoted to these when vacancies occurred. There was, in short, a ladder of promotion from chorister to parish priest and the cathedral was effectively a training-place for local clergy.[34] Many parish churches must have benefited from having as their priest an ex-cathedral man who had been in contact with worship, music and preaching of a high standard.

The cathedral community was thus both large and varied. Numbers fluctuated at different periods, but after 1300 you could normally have counted on finding sixteen to eighteen resident canons, twenty to twenty-four vicars, twelve to twenty-one annuellars, seven to twelve secondaries and fourteen choristers: say seventy to ninety clergy in all. In the Middle Ages, however, no clerical community was purely clerical; even monks had servants, and so did the cathedral clergy. In the Close the clergy were in fact outnumbered by a crowd of unmarried men and boys who served in the canons' houses. Although the occasional miserly canon kept a mere couple of servants,[35] a proper household was reckoned to include at least six, and one or two canons in the fifteenth century had as many as nine.[36] In every period there were probably well over a hundred servants in the Close altogether. They too varied in rank, from squires who acted as stewards and gentlemen-in-waiting, through pages, yeomen and secretarial clerks, down to grooms and ordinary serving-men and boys. A canon's servant had some privileges. Like the cathedral clergy, he came under the authority of the dean for religious purposes, and under that of the bishop – not the mayor – for secular matters. Servants had no status or duties in the cathedral but, like the vicars, they attended their masters to church and followed the clergy in the great processions that went round the city on certain days of the year. The famous brawl of Ascension Day 1445, when the city officers were accused of arresting the chancellor's servant as he held up his master's cope, seems to have arisen because the canons' servants crowded into the procession behind the clergy and in front of the mayor and citizens, who were outraged at being demoted by men of lesser rank.[37] And once a year in June, as we shall see, the servants joined together as a group and had their own festivities on the cathedral green.[38]

A handful of other servants were hired for specific tasks. Each quarter of the year the treasurer paid small retaining fees to a seamstress, a laundress and the pitmaker or grave-digger.[39] The two female servants were the only women employed by the cathedral, but they did not live in the Close or necessarily even work there. Finally, there was one four-legged funtionary: the cathedral cat, who rejoiced in an official status and in his own salary. Included in the cathedral obit accounts for the years 1305 to 1467 is a regular payment of 13d. a quarter 'to the custors and the cat' *(custoribus et cato)*. Once, the payment is said to be 'for the cat' alone *(pro cato)*.[40] Thirteen pence a quarter, 4s. 4d. a year, is exactly a penny a week and it looks as though the custors spent this money on meat to supplement the cat's own pickings from birds and rats. A cat-hole still exists in the door under the clock on the north transept wall; the cat would have come through this to make his rounds in search of furred and feathered pests. It is a pity that the authorities never thought to commemorate him by a carving on a boss or corbel when the cathedral was built. John Catterick, who was appointed bishop in 1419, would probably have introduced some feline decorations, for his coat of arms was 'sable, three cats argent', but he died at Florence before he could even come to Exeter. The omission was eventually remedied when the chapel of St Mary Magdalene and St James was rebuilt after the Second World War. A fine cat's head can now be seen in the chapel. It represents Tom, the cat owned by the head virger of the time, and has only one eye, for Tom lost the other in a fight with an owl for possession of a rat; the rat is also immortalized in a carving near by.

5

The King

Anyone who examines the stone carvings on the cathedral walls soon comes across the sculpture of a king or a queen. There are crowned heads on the corbels, notably under the minstrels' gallery; there is a mysterious seated king in a red gown, flanked by angels, on one of the roof bosses in the nave, and there is a line of kings along the lowest level of the west front. Clearly, kings were powerful images in the fourteenth century, when the cathedral was built. They figured prominently in the Bible, as types of greatness or evil, like David and Herod. They played an important part in the cathedral's own history, as founders and benefactors, like Athelstan and Edward the Confessor. And they were important, perhaps most important of all, in the contemporary world, as rulers of the English people. For whereas the kings of the past lay safely dead and neatly assigned to places in history and symbolism, the kings of the present mattered to everyone. Law and order, peace and war, prosperity and misfortune, all depended on the king's strength or weakness, on his favour or disfavour.

In theory the cathedral, like the medieval Church in general, was largely outside the king's jurisdiction. Officially, the Church was an independent body. It had its own rulers: the pope and the bishops. Its members chose these rulers themselves and governed their own affairs according to their own laws. The Church had liberties which the king could not infringe: sanctuary – the freedom of churches from the king's officers, and benefit of clergy – the right of clerics to be tried for crimes in their own Church courts, not in the courts of the king. In the Church's view the king was not its overlord but its ally and protector, responsible for shielding its members and their property against wrongdoers and for putting its judgments into effect against heretics and sinners. But this was the ideal and not the fact. Ever since there had been a Church in England, kings had disputed the independence of the clergy and encroached on the Church's rights. They interfered with the choosing of bishops and abbots to get the appointments they wanted. They meddled with Church property, demanding dues and taxes from it and even taking control of it for short periods. And they crossed the line between the sacred and the secular by claiming to possess spiritual powers. Each reigning English monarch from Edward I to Queen Anne regularly laid their hands on people to cure them from the disease of scrofula, the 'king's evil'.[1] This was something that even the clergy could not do. No part of the Church was free from royal interference, even before Henry VIII made himself head of the Church in 1534, and the cathedral was no exception. The king was an important influence both on its clergy and its worship and no account of either is complete without him.

Let us begin with the king's influence on the clergy. This is a good example of the gap between theory and practice. The key local figure, as far as the cathedral clergy were concerned, was the bishop, because he appointed all the dignitaries and canons, except for the dean. It is therefore crucial to cathedral history to know who appointed the bishop. The appointment ostensibly belonged to the Church.[2] Up to and including Bishop Berkeley in 1326, all the bishops were elected by the cathedral chapter of dignitaries and canons. Then, in the early fourteenth century, the popes decided to take over the appointment of bishops themselves. At Exeter this happened for the first time in 1327, when Bishop Grandisson was appointed. From that year until the Reformation all the bishops were 'provided' by the pope. Appearances, however, are misleading. On the whole, between 1050 and the Reformation neither the chapter nor the pope made a free choice of bishop; instead they ratified a choice already made by the kings. This becomes clear when we study the bishops' careers. The first three Exeter bishops, Leofric, Osbern and William Warelwast, had all been clerks or chaplains in the royal household. The same was true of Branscombe in the mid-thirteenth century, of Stapledon in the early fourteenth and of all the bishops from Brantingham (in 1370) onwards. Some of these men stayed in the king's service even after becoming bishops. Stapledon and Brantingham were treasurers of England and Stafford and Nevill were chancellors, living in London and running the diocese through deputies. It is manifest from this that the king was the dominant influence on the appointments. Although the evidence does not always survive, it seems that he asked the chapter or the pope to choose his nominees, and they obliged him. There were exceptions to this pattern in the late twelfth century, parts of the thirteenth and the years 1326–7, when royal influence seems to have been weaker and chapter freedom stronger, leading to the appointment of humbler local men. But these cases are in the minority. For the papacy the only truly free choice was the first one, when John XXII provided Grandisson. This was the consequence of an unusual situation. Edward II was being deposed and an insecure regency government was taking over in the name of a new young king. The pope could therefore play a forceful role, for the first and last time, as far as Exeter was concerned.

Most of the bishops of Exeter in the Middle Ages, then, were king's men, not simply the king's nominees, but men who had worked for years in his service. But the king's influence reached a good deal further than this, into the personnel of the cathedral itself. First, he had the right, known as 'regale', to exercise the bishop's non-spiritual powers (including the appointment of canons) when the bishopric was vacant. Between 1300 and 1540, for example, there were sixteen vacancies lasting for a total of over five years, and during these periods successive kings directly appointed at least twenty canons by the right of regale.[3] For the rest of the time, the king or queen could get the bishop to make appointments for them. Thus we hear

44

Emsiquis eris qui tranlieris sta plege plona
ꝼim qᵒeris fuerā oꝛ qᵒes: pꝛo me ꝑecoꝛ oꝛa
Hic iacet Iohēs bolbthe quōdā eps Exonēꝝ qui
Obiit vi die mēsis Aprilis A dni mᵒ cccc lxxviiᵒ

Bishop Bothe
*Bishop John Bothe (d. 1478) was a typical king's appointment of the later
Middle Ages; he had previously been secretary to Edward IV. He died at
East Horsley, Surrey, which belonged to the Bishop of Exeter, and was
buried there.*

that in 1308 Queen Isabella asked Bishop Stapledon to give a canonry to her chaplain John of Jargolio; after a two-year delay (because there was no post immediately available) Stapledon duly made Jargolio a canon.[4] This kind of royal influence is hard to trace, because the letters about it rarely survive. The fact that royal servants became cathedral canons may be due to their friendship with the bishop, as well as to the king's recommendation. But by whatever means, a further number of royal servants got cathedral benefices: men like Richard Bury and Roger Walden in the fourteenth century, and William Lyndwood and Thomas Rotherham in the fifteenth.[5]

Finally, during the fifteenth century, the king extended his influence over the appointment of the dean. The dean was elected by the rest of the canons, and since the deanship was an important and lucrative office, it also attracted the interest of the king and his servants. From 1458, when Henry VI requested the chapter to elect Dr John Hals, most of the deans were royal nominees.[6] Once, in 1509, the chapter refused to elect the Master of the Rolls, John Young, although he had a recommendation from Henry VIII. Young was not a canon (the necessary qualification for election as dean) and the chapter said they could not wait until he was made one.[7] In fact, in a similar case in the previous year, the chapter had waited when pressed to do so by the old king, Henry VII, so perhaps the canons were trying to assert themselves against his new and untried son.[8] But even here, they did not go too far. The man they elected, John Veysey, was also a king's servant, and the bishop gave Young a consolation prize: the archdeaconry of Barnstaple![9]

We would expect a cathedral with royal founders, whose clergy included royal officers, to remember the king in its daily worship. At first sight, the pre-Reformation cathedral services seem to have given him little attention compared with the later Protestant ones. There were no prayers for the king in any of the ordinary daily services except the mass, where the priest prayed during the canon or prayer of consecration for the pope, the bishop, the king and the people.[10] This order reflected the Church's view of its independence from the king and superiority over him. However, since there were over twenty masses a day in the cathedral, the king got a good deal of spiritual benefit from this source, and gradually, from the late thirteenth century onwards, additional royal prayers were introduced. In 1285, when Edward I visited Exeter, Bishop Quinil authorized one such prayer to be said at mass after the consecration, though it is not clear whether it continued to be used when the visit was over.[11] In 1315 the cathedral promised to celebrate the accession day of Edward II with a special mass.[12] The priests of three of the chantries founded in the cathedral were also instructed to pray for the king: those of the Bratton chantry (founded between 1272 and 1277), for the kings of England generally, those of Bishop Brantingham's chantry (1376) for Edward III and Queen Philippa, and those of Bishop Stafford's chantry (1408) for Henry IV and his four sons.[13] There were also obits, or annual memorial masses, for Athelstan, Edward III and Philippa, and the Black Prince.[14] Several of these arrangements reflected personal connections between the clergy and the king, Brantingham having been a servant of Edward III and Stafford of Henry IV, to whom he was also related. The Black Prince's obit was

46

founded by Canon Henry Blakeborn, who had once been treasurer of the prince's wardrobe, and was first observed in 1414.[15]

Prayers at these chantry masses and obits were relatively private and made more impact on the clergy than they did on the people. But the fourteenth and fifteenth centuries saw a parallel increase in public prayers for the king. Some of the impetus for this came from the king himself. Cathedrals played a part in official propaganda in the Middle Ages. In 1279, and again in 1297 and 1300, copies of Magna Carta were ordered to be displayed in all of them for the public to read.[16] In 1355, during the Hundred Years War, Edward III requested Grandisson to arrange prayers and processions throughout the diocese for the king's forthcoming campaign in France. Similar appeals for public prayers were made until the 1440s.[17] And, lest anyone should ask what the war was about, in 1437–8 the king's council told the cathedral to put up a board depicting the royal family trees of England and France to explain Henry VI's claim to the French throne.[18] By the middle of the fifteenth century, a 'bidding-prayer' was read before the high mass on Sundays, when the largest number of people were present in the cathedral. This asked the congregation to pray, in addition to various good causes, for King Alfred, Athelstan, Edgar and all the English kings from the Norman Conquest onwards. After the prayer the clergy said, in Latin, the versicles and responses which we know as 'Endue thy ministers [i.e. the clergy] with righteousness', 'O Lord save the king' and 'O Lord save thy people'.[19] When Cranmer compiled the first English prayer-book in 1549, he had to take account of a long tradition of praying for the king, and (as elsewhere in his work) he tried to tidy things up. He brought the practice into the standard daily services of matins and evensong, as well as the mass, and used as part of his material the versicles and responses mentioned above. By 1549, of course, the king had officially become head of the Church, and Cranmer accordingly changed the order of the versicles to king, clergy and people.

In the Middle Ages, relations between the king and the cathedral were generally carried on at a distance, through letters and prayers. From time to time, however, the two came face to face. Kings and other members of the royal family visited Exeter and saw the cathedral; indeed, on these occasions they often stayed in the houses of the bishop or the other clergy. The history of these visits in the Middle Ages can be roughly divided into two periods.[20] Until the 1340s royal visits were rare. Royalty did not tour the country as impartially as they do today; they merely went where they needed or wanted to go. The South West of England did not often come into either category. It was a peripheral part of the kingdom and one which gave little trouble compared with the other peripheries: Wales and the North. It had scarcely a shrine worth visiting and was unattractive for hunting; the king could enjoy himself as well or better in the forests nearer London. So until the middle of the fourteenth century visits from the king were as infrequent and amazing as the coming of Halley's Comet. William the Conqueror came in 1068 as part of his efforts to gain control over all of his newly won kingdom.[21] Stephen arrived with similar motives in 1136 and captured the castle which was holding out against him. Both kings probably visited the cathedral during their stay, and Stephen (a kind-hearted man) presented the canons with an annuity of £7. 10s. to compensate for damage to their property caused by the siege of the castle.[2] After this there were few or no royal visitors until the reign of Edward I who came three times.

The most important of Edward's visits was in 1285, when he came to see justice done for the precentor's murder and to settle the disputes between the cathedral and the city. It was a planned visit and a family occasion. The party included the queen, Eleanor of Castile, and three of Edward's daughters: Eleanor, Joan and Margaret. There was festivity as well as business, for the two weeks of the visit covered the whole twelve days of Christmas – the only time that a king has ever kept the feast in Exeter. The royal party seem to have stayed in the castle, but there can be little doubt that they visited the cathedral, possibly on Christmas Day itself.[2] Later, in the spring of 1297, Edward passed through the city twice, apparently in order to inspect preparations at Plymouth for an expedition to France.[24] But there is no clear evidence that he did more than pass through on these occasions.

The royal absence from the South West of England began to be remedied in the 1350s. Initially the change was due to the Hundred Years War. The war involved the royal family in much coming and going between England and Europe, including Bordeaux and the surrounding region, which were in English hands throughout the war, and Spain and Portugal, which also saw some of the fighting. Although these places could be reached from various southern ports, the smallness of the ships and the roughness of the Bay of Biscay made royal travellers prefer to go as far as possible by land and to embark (or disembark) at Plymouth. They duly passed through Exeter and had an opportunity of seeing the cathedral.

The first to come was Joan of the Tower, the fourteen-year-old daughter of Edward III. On 29 January 1348 she travelled through the city (where she was entertained by the bishop) on her way to Bordeaux via Plymouth to marry the crown prince of Castile, Pedro the Cruel. The journey was to end in tragedy. The Black Death was already raging in France and the princess caught it after she arrived, dying in Bordeaux on 2 September before her marriage could take place.[25] In the summer of the following year her mother, Queen Philippa, also came to Exeter. She visited the cathedral and offered money at the high altar, probably 13s. 4d. (one mark), although only 13s. is noted in the cathedral accounts.[26] The queen appears to have been touring the West of England rather than making for a port, and this was so unusual that the Black Death, one suspects, was also a factor here. In 1348–9 it may have seemed safer to travel round the provinces than to stay in the vicinity of London.

Philippa's eldest son Edward – the Black Prince – came to the city several times. In 1345 he made a summer tour of his properties in the Duchy of Cornwall, visiting Exeter twice and staying there for over four days on his homeward journey.[27] In May 1357 he landed at Plymouth in triumph with the King of France as his prisoner and both of them rode through Exeter on their way to London.[28] Edward may well have called at the cathedral on these occasions. Later, in 1362, he was appointed Prince of Aquitaine and sent to rule the English lands in France. This brought him back to Exeter another five times as he shuttled between London and Plymouth collecting supplies before sailing from Plymouth in June 1363.[29] The prince was a happy man at this time. He was victorious in war, the ruler of a large new territory and the newly married husband of Joan, the Fair Maid of Kent, who was to bear him two sons.

Eight years later, when the Black Prince came to Exeter for the last time, it was all very different. Things had not gone well for him in France, personally or politically. In 1369 the war had been resumed, shattering the peace of the 1360s, and the French king began to recover the lands which the Black Prince ruled. Unable to arrange the set-piece battles in which he excelled, Edward was reduced to sacking the disloyal town of Limoges and killing its ordinary people. Sickness attacked him – he was never fully to recover – and shortly before Christmas 1370, it struck and killed his eldest son, the seven-year-old Prince Edward. The Black Prince consulted his doctors and was advised to leave for England immediately, with his wife and remaining son, the future Richard II, who was four. They left so hastily, it was said, that they did not even stay to bury Prince Edward. This had to be done by the Black Prince's brother, John of Gaunt.[30] The voyage home in winter cannot have been pleasant, and when they docked at Plymouth at about Christmas, the prince collapsed at Plympton Priory, unable to face the muddy roads to London.[31] Not until Easter was over did the royal party set out, pausing in Exeter on the way. The princess took Prince Richard to the cathedral and they made a splendid offering: 61s. 8d. in the accounts, perhaps more truthfully 66s. 8d. (five marks).[32] The Black Prince is not mentioned in the records and he may have been confined to bed or to a litter. He never came again, and died in 1376, leaving Richard to inherit the throne in the following year.

John of Gaunt returned to England later in 1371. His affairs were a good deal more promising than those of the Black Prince. He had just married his second wife, Constance of Castile, who brought with her a good claim to the throne of her native land. Gaunt subsequently called himself King of Castile and was eventually bought off by the reigning king for a large sum of money. John and Constance left from La Rochelle towards the end of October in a former salt-ship, the *Gaynpayn*, and landed at Fowey in early November.[33] Riding to London, they arrived in Exeter on the 16th, visited the cathedral and offered 20s.[34]

Devon and Exeter played little part in the troubles of the following years – the Peasants' Revolt and the downfall of Richard II – but they did have a chance to see the man who supplanted Richard in 1399: Henry IV, the son of John of Gaunt. Henry came to Exeter in January 1403, the first reigning monarch to do so for over a hundred years. This visit was also linked to the wars in France. Henry, a widower, had decided to marry Joan, the daughter of the King of Navarre. She was herself the widow of the Duke of Brittany, to whom she had borne several children. Henry had six children of his own, however, including four sons, and he seems to have chosen Joan in order to strengthen his links with Brittany, not to enlarge his family. Joan sailed from Brittany on 14 January and landed at Falmouth after five days of storm. Henry rode to Exeter to meet her and they stayed in the city for three days (30 January to 1 February) before leaving for Winchester, where they were married. Once again, it seems likely that a visit to Exeter Cathedral was made, but the king's activities have been recorded only in so far as they involved the mayor and the citizens.[35]

Henry V did not make an appearance in Exeter and half a century passed before the king was again seen in the city. This time, in 1452, it was Henry VI, making what turned out to be the first of six visits by various monarchs in just under fifty years, a total unequalled till modern times. These visits were the result of the internal disorders which we know as the Wars of the Roses. By 1452 Henry VI was already in trouble. His government was unpopular, it was manifestly failing to keep law and order and it had lost nearly all the hard-won English lands in France. In 1450 Cade's rebellion showed the strength of popular discontent and, though this was put down, it forced the king to try to restore public confidence. During the summers of 1451 and 1452 Henry made lengthy tours around the provinces to show himself to his people.[36] The journey of 1452 was planned in advance, which gave the authorities along the route time to make preparations for the king's reception. Henry was met by the nobility and gentry of Devon on 14 July, as he crossed the county boundary from Dorset. After spending three nights in East Devon, he approached Exeter on Monday the 17th and was received in turn by the mayor and citizens at Clyst Honiton, by the friars at Livery Dole and by the rest of the city clergy at the South Gate. The king rode on horseback up South Street, past the city conduit, which was running with wine in his honour, and into the Close through the Broad Gate. Here he found the bishop (the aged Edmund Lacy) and the cathedral clergy waiting to greet him. He dismounted and followed them on foot into the cathedral and up to the high altar, where he prayed and made an offering. During the two nights of his stay Henry lodged in the bishop's palace. On the second day his judges held a trial in the palace and condemned two men to death for treason. This show of strength did not turn out very well. The bishop and the canons complained that the death sentences compromised their rights of sanctuary, and the king was obliged to appease them by pardoning the offenders.[37] A muddle of this kind was hardly a good advertisement for a king who was trying to demonstrate his effectiveness.

Nor, in the long term, did the tour achieve its aim. A year later Henry began to suffer from mental illness and within three his authority was so weak that the Earl of Devon was able to attack the cathedral itself (an episode which will be mentioned in the following chapter). The Wars of the Roses ensued, and in 1461 Henry was ousted from the throne by Edward IV. For the rest of the century there were risings and outbreaks of civil war at least once every decade. Many of these took place in the outlying parts of the kingdom and Devon too played a role in this respect. In 1470 Edward IV fell out with the Earl of Warwick (The Kingmaker) who had helped him take the throne, and with his own brother, George, Duke of Clarence. The king advanced to the North with an army and Warwick, Clarence and their wives fled south to Exeter, Dartmouth and thence overseas. Edward pursued them from York with remarkable speed. He and his forces did the 290-mile journey to Exeter in only eighteen days, but arrived, on 14 April, to find that their prey had escaped.[38] Edward stayed for two nights, however, and on the 15th he and his household joined in the usual Palm Sunday procession of the cathedral clergy through the Close and round the nearby streets.[39] This was an honour for which the cathedral paid dearly, since whatever money the king may have given as an offering was dwarfed by the £74. 3s. 4d. which the chapter felt obliged to give him, £40 of it hastily raised from the pilgrims' donations at Bishop Lacy's tomb.[40] Four months later Warwick and Clarence were back in Exeter, en route for London, and it was Edward's turn to flee abroad. Henry VI was put back on the throne. Then, in the spring of 1471 Edward returned to England, Clarence defected to him and Warwick was killed at the Battle of Barnet. A last attempt to save the cause of Henry VI was made by Queen Margaret of Anjou and her son Edward, Prince of Wales. They crossed from France to Weymouth on 14 April 1471 and reached Exeter towards the end on the month.[41] Again the chapter had to make a gift, this time 100 marks (£66. 13s. 4d.).[42] Margaret and Edward marched from Exeter to Tewkesbury, but they lost the battle there on 4 May. It was the end of Henry's cause and, as it must have seemed, of the Wars of the Roses.

The renewal of the hostilities was due to Richard III's preposterous action in seizing the throne in 1483. A good many royal officials and courtiers found it impossible to stomach the usurpation, and in the autumn of 1483 risings broke out. It is a measure of the disgust that Richard aroused that some of the clergy were themselves moved to join in, led by the Bishop of Exeter (Peter Courtenay), the Archdeacon of Exeter and the Abbot of Buckland. But the risings were badly co-ordinated and Richard III reacted quickly. Having decided to deal with his Devonshire enemies in person, he reached Exeter on about 8 November only to discover, like Edward IV before him, that the bishop and most of his friends had escaped to join the Earl of Richmond (Henry VII) in France. Richard had the temporary satisfaction of staying in the bishop's palace during his visit, but the bishop had the last laugh.[43] He personally witnessed Richard's downfall at Bosworth in 1485 and not only regained his bishopric but became one of Henry VII's chief ministers. Two years later he was promoted to be Bishop of Winchester.

Bosworth is often considered to mark the end of the Wars of the Roses, but this is not wholly true. Henry VII encountered plots in his turn (one of which, as we shall see, was hatched in the cathedral),[44] and two rebellions took place, linked with the names of Lambert Simnel (1487) and Perkin Warbeck (1497). Exeter played a notable part in resisting Warbeck's rising and when it had been crushed, Henry VII came to the city – with Warbeck in tow – [45] to thank the citizens and deal with some of the prisoners. He arrived on 7 October and stayed until 3 November: the last visit by a king in the Middle Ages and the longest ever.[46] Henry lodged in the treasurer's house on the north side of the cathedral. Here a striking ceremony was staged. A large new window was built on the side of the house overlooking the cathedral green and the trees in front of it were cut down. The king stood in the window and the rank-and-file rebels (who were Cornishmen) stood on the green in front of him, bareheaded, with halters round their necks. They cried out to the king to pardon them, and he replied with a short speech, at the end of which he granted their request, whereupon 'the

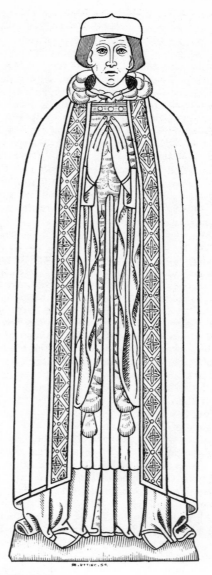

Canon Christopher Urswick

In cap and cope, as he must have looked in church on great occasions. Urswick was one of several clergy who fled from Richard III to join Henry VII, and returned in 1485. He later became both Canon and Chancellor of Exeter Cathedral, dying in 1522.

people made a great shout, hurled away their halters and cried "God save the king!" '.[47] It was an effective piece of theatre and, unlike the pardons of Henry VI, it had the desired result.

With the end of the Wars of the Roses, Exeter ceased to require the monarch's personal presence and things reverted to how they had been before the 1340s. In the sixteenth century neither the city nor the cathedral saw a reigning monarch. It was not till the next great aristocratic revolt (the Civil War) that the king (Charles I) was obliged to travel west as far as Exeter. There was, however, one more visit before the Reformation by a member of the English royal family: Katherine of Aragon. She landed at Plymouth on 2 October 1501 on her way to be married to Prince Arthur.[48] Later, of course, Katherine was to marry his brother, Henry VIII. She travelled slowly and spent several days in Exeter, staying in the deanery and so enjoying the privilege, rare for a woman, of passing the night in the Close. Unfortunately, her stay was not altogether comfortable. It was the time of the equinoctial gales,

... the weather was very foul and windy and full of storms, by reason whereof the weathercock which was upon the steeple of the church of St Mary-the-More [St Mary Major] which is adjoining to the said dean's house, did so whistle that the said princess could not sleep, whereupon order was taken that some one man should climb up and pull it down, which was done but the said man in great danger, and after her departure the same was put up again.[49]

The dean and chapter gave Katherine a present of money; we do not know how much, but it was at least £14.[50] None of them can have known, as she left for London on 17 October, what lay in store for her and, through her, for the Church. For the drama in which she was to play a part, with Henry VIII and the pope, was to be the catalyst of the Reformation in England, and thereby to change the very cathedral itself.

6

The People

For clergy, king and people – so the medieval clergy prayed. We have now seen something of the roles of the clergy and the king in the cathedral, but what of the people? Unlike parish churches, medieval cathedrals were not primarily churches dedicated to serving the people. They were private churches, bishops' churches, staffed by clergy serving God in some seclusion from the everyday world. Even today cathedrals are 'extra-parochial', outside the parish system, and they are under the absolute control of their clergy, without any help from churchwardens or lay councillors. At the same time, they have always attracted great interest from the public. No sooner was Exeter Cathedral established than lay people came to the building to share in its activities. They wanted its relics to heal them, its saints to protect them and its clergy to pray for them. They worshipped at its altars and listened to its services. They also came with motives which were not religious. The poor arrived to beg for charity,[1] criminals ran in, searching for sanctuary, and ordinary folk appeared, as tourists do today, to look around and entertain themselves.

The clergy, for their part, responded to the public's interest and tried to increase it. From a very early date they claimed that the cathedral was not simply a religious house, but the mother church of the diocese.[2] They tried to develop a relationship with everyone who lived in the diocese, just as parish churches did with the people of their individual parishes. In the case of the parish churches, there was a definite obligation on the laity to maintain the church and its clergy through the regular payment of tithes and offerings. The cathedral was not as close to the people as the parish churches, but during the twelfth century it also managed to make the laity support it in two respects. One of these has been mentioned already: the cathedral's rights of funeral and burial in the city of Exeter. Every Exeter layman and woman had to be brought to the cathedral for funeral rites, and all the funeral offerings and payments passed to the cathedral staff.[3] The other was the custom that people throughout the diocese, all over Devon and Cornwall, should make a small offering to the cathedral every year at Whitsuntide. This practice is first mentioned when Bartholomew was bishop (1161–1184),[4] and it was made compulsory by Bishop Henry Marshall (1194–1206). He laid down that each household in the diocese should make an annual Whitsuntide offering of at least a halfpenny, which was either to be given to the cathedral in person or forwarded by the local clergy.[5] Both of these duties remained in force throughout the rest of the Middle Ages and both brought the cathedral a regular but modest supply of money.[6]

The scope for compulsion, however, was rather limited. A large number of people visited the cathedral of their own free will, and there were more opportunities for getting them to part with their money on a voluntary basis. Recognizing this, the clergy spent a good deal of time persuading visitors to come to the cathedral and encouraging them to make offerings. As well as the traditional attractions of the cathedral (relics, altars and services), indulgences were increasingly important in this respect during the later Middle Ages. Indulgences, as we have seen, were documents recommending people to do a specific good work. If you did the work in a devout frame of mind, you were excused a certain number of days of penance (usually forty). We tend to think of indulgences as a device for raising money, but a great many of them (perhaps the majority) did not involve the payment of money at all. In the case of the cathedral, there were indulgences for visiting the building and praying there, as well as for making financial contributions. In 1324, for example, indulgences of forty days were offered to people attending services in the Lady chapel; in 1343, a hundred days to those who worshipped in the cathedral on the feasts of Our Lady and St Edward the Confessor, and in 1425, forty days to those who visited four specific altars.[7] Not all the indulgences that were granted are now known, but the cathedral evidently kept a record of them, and by the early sixteenth century somebody totted them up and reckoned that they totalled fifty-four years and one Lent![8] This was a useful way of attracting visitors. Even the worst sinners could do a lot to atone for their sins by a pilgrimage to the cathedral, provided of course that they did so in a spirit of repentance and in close liaison with their confessors.

The cathedral did not keep a visitors' book, so we know very few of the names of the people who came. But there is no doubt that they were drawn from a broad cross-section of society. Kings and queens arrived occasionally, as we saw in the previous chapter, and the nobility and gentry must have come fairly often. We are told that Thomas, Lord Berkeley made a pilgrimage in 1328 to the tomb of Bishop Berkeley, his uncle,[9] and if we can assume that other people visited the burial-places of their relatives, we can add the Courtenay Earls of Devon, the Stapledons and the Spekes at a gentry level, and several of the leading citizen families of Exeter. The mayor arrived in state from time to time, and so did his colleagues on the city council.[10] Local people in general came to cathedral services, as well as attending their parish churches in the city, and the poor were not absent, for the records show that donations in the collection boxes were sometimes farthings and broken coins, like the proverbial widow's mite.[11] In 1341 we hear of one poor visitor by name: a certain John the Skinner. He got into trouble for falsely claiming a miraculous cure from blindness in the cathedral, which caused the custors to ring the bells in celebration. Later he confessed that he had not been cured, and had hoped to relieve his poverty by getting money.[12]

The records of the money collected in the cathedral boxes show that the number of visitors varied seasonally, as it does today. During the winter, offerings were smaller and probably given mainly by Exeter people, but in the summer they increased as the roads grew better and visitors came from elsewhere.[13] The medieval cathedral, however, cannot have experienced such an influx of summer tourists as happens now. Exeter was in a distant part of England, not yet touched by tourism, and the cathedral did not possess a major shrine like that of St Thomas of Canterbury or Our Lady of Walsingham to attract pilgrims from all over the kingdom. Most of the summer visitors must have been people from Devon and Cornwall, many of them in Exeter on business or travelling through to other places. Relatively few are likely to have come from outside the South West, and those who did were probably in the area for secular reasons too.

Lay people from Exeter, at any rate, were to be found in the cathedral every day throughout the year. On weekdays, early risers attended the Bratton masses in the nave at daybreak before they started work.[14] People with leisure patronized the later services. In 1387 the annuellars were told to celebrate their masses in succession, so that the laity who came to church could hear them at different times, and in 1472 a ten o'clock mass was established for similarly leisured people.[15] On Sundays appreciable numbers of laity were present before and during the high mass at about nine o'clock, so much so that their presence was noticed and provided for. Cathedral services were normally private by nature and involved only the clergy, but on Sunday mornings a few concessions were made to lay onlookers. Bishop Grandisson's Ordinal of 1337 laid down that sermons should be preached 'to the people' before high mass from Advent to Septuagesima, and that the 'people' should be sprinkled with holy water by an acolyte.[16]

By the middle of the fifteenth century it was customary for one of the clergy to read a bidding-prayer in English to the laity, probably before the high mass. The list of institutions, people and causes included in the fifteenth-century bidding-prayers is not dissimilar to modern ones, except in so far as it reflects the doctrines of the Church in the later Middle Ages. First of all, prayers were requested for the pope, the cardinals, the recovery of the Holy Land, for archbishops and bishops, and the cathedral clergy. Next came 'the good state and tranquillity of this land', the king, the queen, all rulers and lords, the common people – especially the mayor and people of Exeter – and all other Christians. Finally, the congregation were asked to remember the benefactors of the cathedral, the souls whose bodies rested inside or in the cemetery, and 'all the souls that abideth the mercy of God in the bitter pains of purgatory, that God of his mercy the sooner deliver them through your devout prayers'.[17] The laity were thus provided with a range of people to pray for while the mass went on.

There are not enough records, unfortunately, to show a detailed pattern of cathedral attendance: the busiest hours or days or the most popular shrines and altars. It is nevertheless clear that the laity were present on most and probably all of the great festivals. There are casual references to offerings of money at the masses on Christmas Night, to people attending the boy-bishop services on 28 December, and to the expulsion of penitent sinners on Ash Wednesday.[18] (We shall also note, later on, the readmission of the penitents on Maundy Thursday and the practice of creeping to the cross by the people on Good Friday.)[19] The laity are known to have accompanied the clergy to the sepulchre at daybreak on Easter Day,[20] and there was a major influx of people during the four days of Whitsuntide when offerings had to be made. Other gifts are recorded on Corpus Christi, 1 August (Lammas Day, the Feast of St Peter in chains) and 29 September (Michaelmas Day).[21] The cathedral contained a dozen or more collecting boxes, attached to particular altars, images and tombs, and records of the box receipts from 1306 to 1467 survive.[22] Regrettably, the totals for individual boxes are not specified and some of the boxes are left out, so we can only guess which ones (and therefore which altars and images) were most popular with the laity. It seems probable, however, that people liked to gather at the east end of the nave, in the crossing and the transepts, and that a good deal of money was put into the boxes in this area, especially the one by Old Peter, which received the offerings for the cathedral fabric.

The cathedral had no saint or relic of national importance, but, as we saw in Chapter 3, it contained the tombs of two men who were locally regarded as holy, and these were also well attended by visitors.[23] The first was that of Bishop Berkeley, whose fame sprang up immediately after his death in 1327. Until about the time of the Black Death, in 1348–9, numerous pilgrims came to his tomb in the choir to light candles and offer money. Later on enthusiasm cooled, visitors ceased to come and by the end of the fourteenth century the cult of Bishop Berkeley was quite extinct. In the following century there was a similar outburst of devotion at the tomb of Bishop Lacy. Edmund Lacy was bishop for thirty-five years and died in 1455 in his mid-eighties, an aged and venerable figure. He was a devout man who did much to increase the worship of Our Lady and the archangels Gabriel and Raphael, and well before his death he had acquired a reputation for 'blessedness, holy living and good conscience', as the Mayor of Exeter expressed it. His body was buried in the choir opposite Berkeley in an equally plain tomb, which suggests that Lacy saw himself (or was seen by other people) as Berkeley's successor. In due course the tomb began to be visited by pilgrims. They prayed to Lacy to ask God to heal their bodily ailments, and some were cured, or thought they were, for Hooker (writing in later, Protestant times) tells us that many miracles were 'said or devised to be done' by the bishop's help. Wax models were hung up at the tomb on bits of string to represent the pilgrims or their afflicted parts, probably as reminders to Lacy of the cures they wanted. A cache of these models was discovered in 1943, hidden in the masonry above the tomb. It included images of people, human legs and feet, and the heads and limbs of horses.[24] Lacy himself had suffered from a disease of the legs and people seem to have thought that he would take a special interest in cases of this kind.

If we could see our ancestors at their devotions in the medieval cathedral, we would be surprised at their behaviour. In the first place, everybody wore headgear in church, chiefly hoods until the evolution of hats in the fifteenth century. It was humiliating to appear bareheaded, as five laymen were made to do in 1383 as part of a penance;[25] normally, hoods were removed in church only in the presence of important people or especially holy objects. You took off your hood during mass, for example, when the priest held up the consecrated wafer and chalice to signify that they had become the body and blood of Christ. A group of Lollard knights elsewhere in England who refused to bare their heads at this point were called 'the hooded knights' as a result.[26] We would also be struck by the general lack of order in the

medieval cathedral, which made the laity at services look more like a crowd
than a congregation. In church nowadays people sit in a clearly designated
area. They all sit together, regardless of rank or sex, and everyone does
much the same thing at the same time, be it singing, praying, standing or
reading. Medieval worshippers were not so well organized. Seating was not
generally provided, so people placed themselves how and where they chose,
standing or sitting on portable seats which they brought with them. When
the clergy passed around the church in procession, it was necessary for the
custors to go in front with staffs and move obstructors out of the
way.[27] The people probably assembled in several different groups, too,
reflecting their social distinctions. Gentlefolk may well have been admitted
into the choir, but if they were in the nave, they would have been
surrounded by their retainers. Citizens probably drew together by rank or
trade, and women gathered in separate groups or were chaperoned.

The congregation did not all do the same thing during services, either. In
modern churches worship is a partnership between the clergy and the laity.
They are both stationed in the same area, they take part in the same
prayers and hymns, and the clergy lead the service so as to bring about a
unified response from the people. In medieval times it was quite otherwise.
The clergy performed the service by themselves and the people were
onlookers, separated from the clergy by the choir-screens and from a literal
understanding of the service by the fact that it was in Latin. Devout lay
people listened to the service and prayed while it went on, but their prayers
were different from those of the clergy – a practice hard for us to

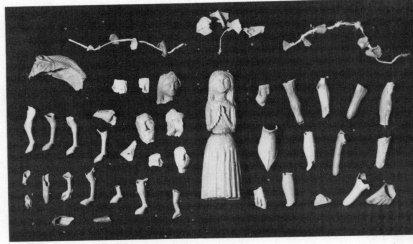

The Wax Images from Bishop Lacy's Tomb
*In 1943 a hoard of images which pilgrims had hung up at the tomb was
found. Left, animal legs and hooves; right, human fingers, legs and feet
representing the cures the pilgrims wanted for themselves and their
livestock.*

understand. Their prayers also differed from one another's, because they were not being led and because they were different in their intellectual capabilities. Wealthy people who could read took prayer-books to church with them. Sometimes they owned Latin breviaries and psalters like the clergy used, and followed the words of service as the clergy said them. In 1327 a breviary and psalter were kept chained in the choir 'to serve the people', possibly so that important lay people could stand in the choir and read them.[28] Other people had simpler prayer-books called 'primers' or 'books of hours', in Latin or English, and read these during the service. An Italian visitor to England in about 1500 noticed that people took such books of hours to church and read them over, 'verse by verse, in a low voice'.[29] Those who could not read prayed extempore or said the prayers they knew by heart, often again and again. Everyone was supposed to know the Lord's Prayer, the Hail Mary and the Apostles' Creed; in 1514 Bishop Oldham mentions the laity saying the first two of these during services.[30] So the organized singing and reading in the choir was accompanied by an unorganized mutter of prayers from the people outside. A mutter, because they tended to read and pray aloud, not silently. And the lack of supervision from the clergy made it easy to be inattentive, talk or even laugh. If a modern congregation can be likened to a class with a teacher, a medieval one was sometimes like a class when the teacher is out of the room.

The people showed their piety not only through their prayers but through their gifts. A stream of dues and offerings flowed from their purses into the cathedral coffers during the later Middle Ages. The fullest evidence about this money comes from the early fourteenth century, between about 1306 and 1345.[31] During this period there were five main kinds of offerings by the laity, most of them varying in their annual yields. For simplicity, we will give rough averages: 1. The compulsory offerings at Whitsuntide, producing about £10 a year. About half of this was deposited in the cathedral itself (probably by Exeter people) and the rest was sent in via collectors who kept part of it for themselves. 2. Offerings at funerals, producing at least £3 a year – probably more, because the receipts are badly recorded. 3. Offerings in the cathedral collection boxes. These were made all the year round, but especially on Corpus Christi and Lammas Day, and averaged about £9 – £10. 4. After 1327, offerings at the tomb of Bishop Berkeley. These reached a peak of about £28 – £35 in the following year, and then declined to about £10 a year in the 1330s and 1340s. 5. Indulgence offerings, made specifically for the fabric of the cathedral, which produced about another £25 a year by the 1320s. There were also unrecorded moneys: offerings at the Lady chapel and one or two of the cathedral altars, sales of candles and fees for ringing the bells at funerals. If we add a notional £5 to cover these, the total income from lay offerings in the early 1320s reaches £50–£60, rising to about £80 in 1328, then sinking back to about £60–£70 in the 1340s. As the fourteenth century wore on, there were changes in the relative size of the offerings. Those at Whitsun gradually fell to £5 – £6 by 1400 and collecting-box receipts to £6–£7, but indulgence revenue increased to over £40 a year, so that the total income from offerings remained in the region of £60–£70. This was a sizeable sum, equal to the wages of all twenty-one annuellars before the Black Death, for example.

Nowadays, as well as visiting the cathedral and attending services, you
can join associations such as The Friends of Exeter Cathedral and The
Cathedral Fellowship which bring you into a closer relationship. There were
associations of a kind in the Middle Ages, too. As early as the late eleventh
century, we hear of guilds of lay people in the Devon countryside linked to
the cathedral by prayer and money. A document copied into the famous
Exeter Book of Anglo-Saxon poetry relates that eighteen people in
Woodbury agreed to pay the cathedral a penny a household every Easter
and a penny whenever one of their members died. In return the cathedral
adopted them into fellowship, which probably means that the clergy
regularly prayed for them along with the other cathedral benefactors. The
same document lists thirteen other guilds with a similar relationship
mainly from places in East Devon, with a total membership of over 300.[3]
In those early times the cathedral was the major church of the surrounding
area, but after the twelfth century, when the parish system was organized
people were expected to relate to their parish churches rather than to the
cathedral, and these local guilds appear to have died out.

The principle of fellowship remained, however, and from the thirteenth to
the sixteenth centuries we occasionally hear of lay people – royalty, gentry
and common people – being granted 'fraternity' with the cathedral and
sometimes paying money for the privilege.[33] By the sixteenth century
printed handbills were produced, encouraging people to become brothers
and sisters of the cathedral. According to the handbills, brotherhood could
be obtained by giving money or goods to the repair of the building. Each
person who did so would benefit from all the cathedral's indulgences: the
fifty-four years and one Lent, all the masses celebrated there, and special
prayers said regularly for all brothers and sisters.[34] This fellowship
fraternity or brotherhood does not seem to have been an organization, like
the present-day Friends of the Cathedral; it did not have officers o
meetings. It is not even clear whether the clergy kept names of the
members; they may well have prayed for them in general terms
Brotherhood was simply a privilege, invisible but valuable, which
channelled spiritual benefits from the cathedral's prayers and worship t
the brothers and sisters.

So far we have looked at the laity in their role as worshippers and money
givers, but this is not the whole story. Some of them came to the cathedra
with quite different motives, for medieval people (like people today) were b
no means all devout or always pious, but often the reverse. The clergy hav
always insisted that the cathedral is a holy place, but many lay people kno
better. It is really a sort of large theatre, open all day, offering shelter fro
the rain, amusements of a sort and costing no money if you are firm enoug
with yourself. In the Middle Ages many people took advantage of thes
things, Exonians as well as visitors, and the cathedral was used for a
kinds of secular purposes: to meet friends, to do business and probably eve
to carry on love affairs.[35] One medieval treatise on the education of gir
actually warned against having sex in church, but that must have bee
difficult in a well-frequented one like the cathedral.[36] However, you cou
safely arrange a conspiracy, as John Hayes, a Tiverton gentleman, did wi
John Taylor, a dedicated Yorkist plotter, in about 1491. This was real cloa

and-dagger stuff: Taylor came up to Hayes in the cloister, a popular place for walking about, and grasped him by the thumb. At this pre-arranged signal they both went into the church to plot the overthrow of the king (Henry VII) and his replacement by the Yorkist candidate, the Earl of Warwick.[37] Criminals came to the building as well as conspirators: thieves, vandals and felons in search of sanctuary.[38] We can still see the remains of the screens and railings which were needed to protect the choir, the altars and the tombs, but neither screens nor fear of God were absolute deterrents to wrongdoers. In Grandisson's time the very pyx, the box which held the consecrated wafer – the holiest object in the church – was stolen from above the high altar.[39]

Nor was the building troubled only by sly thieves; the ruffian and rioter forced his way in too, from time to time. There were several violations of the cathedral by armed men during the later Middle Ages, although it is true that they were rather unusual events, shocking in part for that reason. On All Saints' Day in 1338 a cleric named William le Gyldene came into the cathedral accompanied by men with weapons while a service was going on and made violent demonstrations to force the chapter to instal him as a canon.[40] He obviously made an impact, since he gained possession of a canonry for a time and was eventually bought out by the other person who claimed it. In 1355 there was a spilling of blood in the cathedral, apparently due to a fight between two laymen, and the angry bishop (Grandisson) ordered services to be suspended for two or three days as a warning to the public.[41] In 1383 a criminal sheltering in the cathedral was taken out by force, and in the middle of the fifteenth century there were two or three more violations, reflecting the breakdown of order under Henry VI which led to the Wars of the Roses.

The latter period saw blows between the clergy and the city officers,[42] an attack by men with swords on John Giffard, a local Justice of the Peace, in 1444,[43] and a series of affrays by Sir Thomas Courtenay, son of the Earl of Devon, and his men in 1455. This was at the time when the earl was waging a private war against his enemy Lord Bonville which was to culminate in a pitched battle on Clyst Heath. Courtenay wanted the goods of one of Bonville's allies which had been stored in the cathedral for safety, and he threatened to break down the doors if the clergy resisted. The dean and chapter yielded, leaving the doors open so that Courtenay could help himself. Perhaps they would have done better to show fight, for Courtenay and his men went on to extort money from the dean with menaces, and finally carried off Canon John Morton as he celebrated Sunday mass in the choir, releasing him only when he paid them a ransom. This was probably the worst outrage in the cathedral's history, next to the murder of the precentor, but it happened at a very disturbed time. The bishop had just died, the king was mad, and there was no retribution such as there had been in 1285. In fact, Courtenay survived to become Earl of Devon, and he was executed for other reasons after the Battle of Towton in 1461.[44]

Perhaps the most interesting violation was the one of 1383.[45] On 7 January in that year a leading Devon knight, Sir John Dinham, was attacked and killed by robbers, apparently in Somerset. Two men, John Broun and Robert Tuwyng, were arrested for the crime and taken to

Ilchester gaol, but they escaped, and the dead man's son, a bold young man in his twenties who was also called Sir John, decided to take the law into his own hands. He and his servants tracked down Tuwyng and killed him, but Broun took sanctuary in Exeter Cathedral. Fearful lest Broun should escape again, Sir John went into the cathedral, dragged him out, and took him off to safe custody until he could be properly tried. No doubt there was much sympathy for Dinham's actions, but there was also a resolute bishop, Thomas Brantingham, who was determined that the breach of sanctuary should not go overlooked. Dinham was told to restore the fugitive to the cathedral, and he and his men were all required to do penance for their deed. The penances were carefully graduated according to the rank of those involved. Sir John himself was made to attend the cathedral high mass on a Sunday and to stand bareheaded near the high altar throughout the service holding a lighted candle weighing 2 lb. His squire was ordered to attend high mass on three Sundays, without his hood, cloak or belt, and to stand in the nave throughout the service with a 1-lb candle. And four of the knight's men were required not only to attend on three Sundays but to walk round the church in front of the Sunday procession, without hoods, cloaks, belts or shoes, and to stand throughout the mass with candles weighing ½ lb. In this way Brantingham proclaimed the might of the Church and the inviolability of sanctuary. He also nicely calculated matters. The knight was given the heaviest candle but the most private penance, and the weight of public humilation fell on those who had least to lose: his ordinary followers!

7

The Day

The people of Exeter knew their cathedral by sound, as well as by sight. Nine times a day, and more often on special days, it spoke to the city through the bells in its towers. Sometimes a single bell would ring, sometimes a pair, and sometimes several would clamour and clash at random, as they still do in the campaniles of Europe. There were eventually thirteen bells, five in the north tower and eight in the south. Many of them had names.[1] In the thirteenth century, when French was widely spoken in England, some of these names were French: Chanterel (the little singer), Salterel (the dancer) and Clerematyn (a clear bell for matins). Others had Christian names: Jesus and Mary, Magdalene, Peter and Trinity; others again were called after bishops. There was a Walter bell, a Stafford bell and, greatest of them all, the mighty 2-ton Grandisson, which shook the belfry as its namesake had done the diocese.[2] The ringing was done by the four custors or virgers. They tolled the bells for funerals and rang them with joy for festivals, or to salute the bishop or the king. But oftenest they warned of the approach of services, and so predictably that citizens could tell the time and organize the day by the noise they made.

At the sound of the service bell, the clergy made their way towards the choir. They came from all directions, singly and in groups. The annuellars were free to come and go individually, because they had no masters, but whenever their canons attended the vicars had to accompany them.[3] Each canon went in convoy, with his household staff about him, like all important people in those days, to display his status to the world at large. It was a sombre crowd that gathered, all in black with flashes of white. The normal choir-dress of the Exeter Cathedral clergy was a white surplice, covered by a long black cloak which reached to the feet, and a black cap. This was worn on most days of the year, the chief exception being Easter week, when the clergy abandoned their cloaks and wore only their surplices, whitening the choir in a symbolic gesture to the season.[4] As he entered the choir, each cleric bowed to the high altar and then to the bishop or dean if they were present. Punctators were stationed to watch who came. These were members of the minor clergy, armed with lists of names, who recorded all the absentees.[5] Canons who stayed away had their daily allowance docked, and minor clergy were fined or summoned before the chapter to be punished. Each person took his place on one of the grades of the choir. At

THE CHOIR OF EXETER CATHEDRAL
IN THE MIDDLE AGES

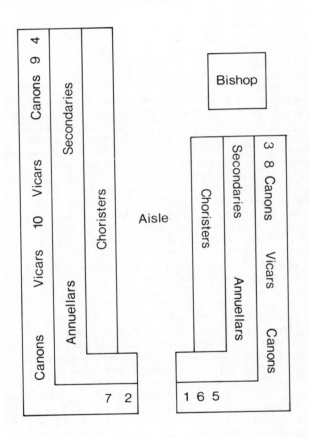

1   Dean
2   Precentor
3   Chancellor
4   Treasurer
5   Subdean

6   Archdeacon of Exeter
7   Archdeacon of Cornwall
8   Archdeacon of Totnes
9   Archdeacon of Barnstaple
10 Succentor

The Choir of Exeter Cathedral

the four corners of the top level were the four chief dignitaries: dean, precentor, chancellor and treasurer, the cornerstones of the cathedral. Beside them on the top level or 'third form,' as it was also called, were the canons and vicars, with the annuellars and secondaries below them in the second form, and the choristers on the lowest level or first form. The table opposite shows the layout, which was almost the same as the modern one.[6]

The core of the staff of the choir consisted of the vicars, annuellars and secondaries. They had to attend all the daily services, of which there were nine, unless they were ill or granted leave of absence.[7] Leave was not often given, except for a pilgrimage or an important piece of private business, and the chapter had to give formal approval on each occasion.[8] The canons, on the other hand, were privileged to be absent for much of the time. Some of them did not even live in Exeter and those who did were obliged to attend only two services each day, high mass and matins or vespers, in order to qualify for their daily allowances.[9] The choristers were another special category. They were required to be present at all services on Sundays and major festivals, but on ordinary days most of them spent several hours in school learning to read and sing, and it was considered sufficient if four or five were in the church at any one time. We would expect children to be given a lighter work-load than their seniors, but this was not the case before the Reformation, and the total time that the choristers spent in school or in the choir was not far short of the adult working day. There were no formal arrangements for them to have playtime; indeed, Bishop Grandisson laid down that 'they should always be engaged in some good task'.[10] In all the number of clergy present in the choir was smaller than the total number of cathedral clergy. The maximum was probably over seventy, at feasts like Christmas and Easter in the early fourteenth century, when recruitment was good. On ordinary days after the Black Death, when the ranks of the clergy were depleted, the number may often have fallen to just over forty.

How were the clergy organized in the choir? On many days of the year the services were straighforward enough, and the participants sufficiently experienced, for the work to go ahead without much preparation. The clergy chanted the psalms, sang the hymns and intoned the prayers with minimal supervision from the precentor (if he was present) or his deputy, the succentor. The two sides of the choir took turns to lead and to respond, alternating every week.[11] On Sundays and important saints' days, however, when the usual framework changed and the music was more complicated, the choir was 'ruled' by two of the minor clergy; on more important days, by four vicars, and on the nineteen most important days, by two canons and two vicars.[12] The 'rulers' or rectors were stationed on opposite sides of the choir, probably in the aisle. They sat on special revolving wooden seats covered with white leather and held boxwood staffs ornamented with silver.[13] Their job was to know beforehand what variable material was to be sung, and to 'enjoin' it by quietly singing the opening notes as a guide to the clergy who had to sing it.

Particular pieces of music were assigned to particular people, as were the reading of lessons, the duty of acting as priest, deacon and subdeacon at the high mass, and special functions during processions. The responsibility for allocating these tasks belonged to the precentor and the chancellor. The precentor (or the succentor) chose the rulers, singers, readers and ministers for mass and made sure that they knew what to do.[14] The chancellor heard the lesson-readers practise beforehand and corrected their mistakes.[15] Each Saturday the rota was fixed for the coming week, and every day the next day's duties were read out as a reminder.[16] By the sixteenth century, the rota had begun to be written down and we have a fragment of one which runs from Easter to early July in 1518. The adjoining table shows what a complex task it was to organize the duties for a great festival like Easter Day.[17]

Most of the clergy generally stayed in their places in the choir during services. They were not wholly stationary, for they stood, sat, knelt and turned to face eastwards, but they spent far more time standing up than doing anything else. Sitting down was reserved for parts of the long night service of matins, parts of the high mass in the middle of the morning, and the whole of the service for the dead in the early afternoon.[18] As the daily round of services lasted for several hours, it is easy to understand how irksome they sometimes became and what a blessing it was to be able to rest your bottom on the misericord, that 'merciful' little shelf under the tipped-up seat. Nor is it surprising that good discipline could not be kept day in, day out, that people's attention wandered and that tricks and pranks were played. In 1330 Grandisson said of the cathedral clergy that some had 'their bodies in the choir but their hearts in the market-place, or the street, or in bed', so that they sang the services negligently and fraudulently. Others, he said, were guilty of bursts of laughter and insolent behaviour. Worst of all, during matins, when there were candles, the clergy at the back of the choir dropped hot wax on the heads of those below.[19] It is not likely that services were always as disorderly as this, but equally, given the failings of human nature, they were not always solemn and beautiful, although no doubt they did succeed in being so on many occasions.

Let us now turn from the choir-stalls and their occupants to the framework of time. When, and for how long, did the clergy come into the choir, and what was the pattern of the cathedral day? It is difficult to know precisely what the clergy do with their time today, let alone what they did in the Middle Ages. We have in principle an excellent guide to the medieval services at Exeter and the organization of the day. This is Grandisson's Ordinal, the handbook he drew up in 1337 to define how the services should be carried out and what they should include. The book was not entirely of his own invention; what he did was to summarize the cathedral's existing customs and suggest a few alterations to bring them into line with practices elsewhere. It is our best account of worship in the cathedral before the Reformation, though we need to remember that the forms of worship did not remain static and that there were changes and developments after 1337 which are not recorded in the Ordinal. Difficulty arises because, by our standards, it does not give much of a sense of the time of day. We measure the day by the clock and it is natural for us to time the tasks that we do by the hours, a.m. and p.m. The cathedral possessed a clock by 1284,[20] but when Grandisson was writing, in 1337, people had not begun to reckon the day in clock hours. Grandisson once refers to a service taking place at 'the third hour of the natural day';[21] occasionally he mentions services in relation

DUTY ROTA FOR EASTER SUNDAY, 1518

Rectors of the choir .... Chancellor and treasurer

Matins

Invitatory, sung by .... Four archdeacons

First respond, sung by .... Meltam, Shebroke, Doke
(vicars)

Second respond, sung by .... Kenwode and Young
(vicars)

Third respond, sung by .... Four archdeacons

High Mass

Second Lesson in Chapter
    House, read by .... Shebroke (vicar)

Processional hymn,
    Salve Festa Dies, sung by .... Heynson, Shebroke and Bynks
(vicars)

At the crucifix on the
    choir-screen .... The same vicars

Aspersions .... Derke and Gyrmow
(annuellars)

Epistle, read by .... Rode (vicar)

Gradual, sung by .... Vicars who sing first respond
at second vespers

Gospel, read by .... Dauson (vicar)

Celebrant .... Bishop or dean

Vespers

Cross, carried by .... Tyson and Cruse (secondaries)

Text, carried by .... More and Northbroke
(secondaries)

Oil and chrism, carried by .... Smyth and Tremyllyon
(secondaries)

to midnight, dawn, dinner-time or sunset, but usually he does not identify a time at all.

In this respect the bishop was typical of Englishmen up to about the fifteenth and sixteenth centuries. Their days were basically defined by dawn and sunset, and what they did within each day was shaped by custom and instinct rather than the clock. Their daily habits were more flexible than ours and changed more as the seasons changed. Labourers rose earlier from March to October, worked longer hours and got more pay than they did in the rest of the year. The clergy too, as we shall see, varied the pattern of their daily services from summer to winter. Our modern practice of living each day in the same way, according to clock time, is a development which dates from the end of the Middle Ages. We first encounter it at the cathedral in 1394, when the chapter laid down that the morning services should normally end at 10 a.m. or an hour later on fasting days.[22] In the fifteenth century clocks became more common throughout England and by the early sixteenth, Exeter people were quite familiar with them, so that we find them talking about the cathedral six o'clock mass and ten o'clock mass, just as we might today about the eight o'clock communion or the 6.30 evensong.[23] As a result, we possess a few references to the hours of services in the period just before the Reformation and these allow us to make some guesses about the approximate daily pattern in Grandisson's time.

The cathedral day began at midnight, with the ringing of the bell for matins. If any Exeter citizen heard the bell as he lay awake in bed, it must have prompted comfortable thoughts: a layman could have his fill of sleep while a cathedral cleric had to rise and dress for work after only a few poor hours of rest. Matins was meant to be a night service and for most of the year it was sung in the dark, by candle-light.[24] In the spring and the summer, however, this practice was modified. During Easter week matins was sung at dawn, in keeping with the symbolism of the Easter services. After Easter, as the nights grew shorter, it was difficult to get any sleep before the service. For this reason, from the Sunday after Easter until Trinity Sunday, matins was postponed until about two o'clock in the morning, so as to finish just before dawn, and on five important summer festivals when it was longer and more elaborate than usual it was brought forward to sunset so that sleep could be taken afterwards.

Matins was the longest and most important of the daily services, apart from high mass; it included biblical lessons as well as psalms, hymns and prayers, and took an hour or more to complete. It was immediately followed by three other services: lauds, the second of the major daily services, and the matins and lauds of Our Lady, which were shorter versions of matins and lauds in praise of the Virgin Mary.[25] Together these four night services formed a block of devotions lasting between an hour and a half and two hours, depending on the importance of the day and the amount of special material that had to be got through. When they were over, some of the clergy went back to bed. This is revealed by an order in April 1387 that matins be postponed till dawn throughout the following summer, because the vicars choral, whose college was being constructed in Kalendarhay, could not rest 'for the noise of the works'.[26] Evidently the workmen started whistling and hammering at daybreak, making a second sleep impossible.

Not everyone retired to bed, however, at least not for very long. As soon as dawn broke, the cleric who acted as porter of the Close had to be up to unlock the Close gates, so that citizens could come in.[27] At the same time, the two annuellars of the Bratton chantry took up their stations at St Mary's altar under the choir-screen to celebrate the first masses of the day for early worshippers. The other annuellars were probably the next to appear; they each had to celebrate mass at one of the small side-altars, which they were permitted to do as soon as the Bratton masses were over.[28] Evidence dating from the sixteenth century suggests that the Bratton masses were said at about five or six o'clock,[29] while the rest of the chantry masses took place between six and eight.[30] At about seven, a group of fourteen vicars, secondaries and choristers began to come on duty to perform the morning round of services in the Lady chapel.[31] These services involved the singing of the short matins, lauds and other 'hours' of Our Lady, followed by the celebration of the Lady mass in her honour. As this mass was proceeding, the bell began to ring for prime, the first of the daytime services in the choir. This followed the Lady mass at about 7.45, and was attended by all the minor clergy and probably some of the canons. Everyone who had to be was now on duty again.[32]

Prime lasted for about thirty-five minutes. When it was over the clergy left the choir in procession and went to the chapter house for 'chapter', which was partly a business meeting and partly a kind of service. It began with a chorister announcing the calendar information for the next day: the date according to the Roman calendar, the age of the moon and the names of the saints to be commemorated. (This practice had fallen into disuse by the sixteenth century, perhaps because printed calendars of the Church year had become easily obtainable, and it was possible to read up what was about to happen.)[33] Next, a secondary read the rota of duties for the following day and if it was a Saturday, the clergy were assigned their duties for the coming week. Then came prayers for the king, for the parents and friends of the clergy and for the dead, after which the meeting broke up. The dean and canons stayed to deal with chapter business. Errant members of the minor clergy in particular were called up at this point to be cautioned or disciplined. Meanwhile, a dozen of the vicars and others departed to celebrate what was called the 'capitular' mass or mass *in capitulo*. This was the first of the two corporate masses of the day and was probably said at the high altar. Normally, it was a requiem mass for the dead, but on saints' days, vigils of important feasts, Sundays and funeral days it was an ordinary mass. The remainder of the minor clergy had a few minutes' break at this point, until this mass was over and the senior clergy came back from the chapter house.[34]

At about nine o'clock, everyone gathered again in the choir for the rest of the morning services: terce (or undern), sext, nones and the high mass.[35] The first three of these were short devotions made up mainly of psalms, and there was some variation in the arrangements for saying them. In winter the order was terce, sext, high mass and nones, all sung in turn in the choir. On Sundays and festivals, however, there was a procession of the clergy round the church between terce and sext, and if a sermon was preached, this too was placed between the procession and sext. The high mass was so called because it was the chief mass of the day, celebrated with the greatest ceremony and with the largest number of clergy present. A priest, deacon and subdeacon were appointed from the clergy in turn, and they wore mass vestments coloured according to the season of the year instead of choir garments. If there was a funeral or an obit, the high mass was brought forward to replace the capitular mass after prime and the funeral or obit mass took the place of the high mass. On most days the morning services ended with nones at about ten o'clock, but in Lent they were extended. Nones was then said before high mass, and vespers was moved from the afternoon to follow high mass, which lengthened the services by a further hour.[36] In 1472 an additional ten o'clock mass was instituted, to be said by an annuellar in the chapel of St Paul, when the services in the choir finished, presumably.[37] This mass was probably introduced for the benefit of leisured citizens who wanted to be able to attend a later mass than the nine o'clock high mass. Late-morning masses were popular in towns at this time and friaries often provided them; in fact, the Exeter Franciscan friary had instituted a ten o'clock mass by 1436.[38] The late mass in the cathedral may well have been an attempt to keep up with the friars, with whom there was always a certain rivalry for the affection and support of local people.

Morning service over, it was time for dinner. This may seem very early to us now, but in the fifteenth century it was common for the aristocracy to dine at ten or eleven o'clock; the servants who attended them at dinner ate even earlier. The meal was over by midday and then the afternoon, or evening, as it was more usually called, began. Unfortunately, we know very little about the times of services during this part of the day. In the later fourteenth century, nones was postponed until after dinner in summer, thereby becoming the first of the afternoon services.[39] This seems to have been a development subsequent to Grandisson's time and we do not know how this nones fitted into the afternoon services which he describes in his Ordinal. These consisted of four units, all of which took place in the choir. First came the office of prayers for the dead (placebo and dirige); next vespers (or evensong), a long service approaching an hour, replaced in Lent by a service called 'collation'; then the shortened vespers of Our Lady and finally compline. This afternoon block of services began at two or three o'clock and lasted for one and a half or two hours. Afterwards, the minor clergy appointed to serve in the Lady chapel went there to say the evening round of services, consisting of the vespers and compline of Our Lady, and the choristers departed to the chapel of St Paul and sang an antiphon, also in praise of the Virgin Mary. Everyone else had to say the compline of Our Lady too, but not necessarily in the choir.[40]

The clergy's work was now complete and they could go home to their suppers at about four or five o'clock. The gates of the Close stayed open for a few hours longer. In the 1440s they were shut at seven in summer, apparently, but in 1511 they were left open till eight in winter and nine in summer.[41] At about nine o'clock the bell rang for curfew.[42] This was the warning, as the name implies, that everyone should 'cover the fire' and damp it down for the night. And so the clergy went to bed, for their first sleep, which would be brought to a close by the matins bell and the start of another day.

How many hours had they spent in church? On a normal day the adult minor clergy – the vicars, annuellars and secondaries – were there for five or six hours, rising to seven or eight on major festivals. The choristers worked for almost as long, partly in choir and partly in school, and only the canons got away with a mere couple of hours. They, however, as clergy, were still expected to say the daily round of services and merely had the privilege of doing so in their own houses. Like most occupations, the work of the clergy could be both rewarding and wearisome. On the positive side, each service was an act of worship that invited its participants to exert themselves in a spiritual way. It was a musical performance, with singers and organs; a poetry recital, based on psalms and hymns, and a history lesson, centred on readings from the Old Testament and the lives of the saints. It was a drama, with actors in costume at the mass, rulers who acted as prompters, and a chorus, all of whom engaged in dialogue and movement full of symbolic meaning. The choir was a school as well, with the rulers as teachers and the clergy arranged in forms; indeed, a third of the clergy consisted of boys and youths being trained for adult clerical life. All this made it a place of intellectual stimulation. But equally, the hours were long and the work repetitive, and the rules, rotas, attendance-marking and time-keeping could become monotonous. Choir took up most of the day, and when meals and domestic activities were allowed for, there was not very much time left. Festival days, which for the laity were holidays, brought extra duties for the clergy, and it was seldom permissible to be absent. As we shall see, there were some feasts and celebrations during the year, but these were rare and much of their brightness came from contrast with the everyday routine.

8

The Year

In the previous chapter we tried to explain what happened at the cathedral on every day of the year. But that is only part of the story. The medieval Church did not observe each day in exactly the same way; on the contrary, it was sensitive to the passing of yearly (as opposed to daily) time, much more so then than it became after the Reformation. There were special observances for the seasons of the Church year: Advent and Christmas, Lent and Easter. There were others for saints' days, and half the days of the year were dedicated to one saint or another. It would be tedious to recount the variations in the services on all these occasions, but we can give an idea of the variety of the cathedral's year by looking at a dozen or so of the great festivals, from Christmas to midsummer. All of these festivals were accompanied by picturesque ceremonies in church, some of which spilled over into the world outside. It has always been the nature of Church festivals to give rise to secular feasts, for holy days to lead to holidays, and the cathedral year included social customs – eating, drinking, and games of various kinds – as well as religious ones.

Christmas is the Church's feast of midwinter. It is also, more than any other Christian festival, the celebration of a night rather than a day. The medieval arrangements for the Christmas services tried to express this fact, just as ours do today. The clergy, of course, were used to performing services at night throughout the year, since matins was usually said in the early hours of the morning. On the night before Christmas, however, not only was cathedral matins said at night but mass was celebrated too – the only time in the year when this was done. This custom is copied by the modern midnight mass. In order that the first mass of Christmas should be celebrated as early as possible on 25 December, the matins of Christmas Day was brought forward to 10 p.m. on Christmas Eve.[1]

The Christmas matins included one special and very beautiful ceremony. Soon after it had started, while the first lesson was being read, a chorister dressed in a plain white gown (or alb) appeared through one of the doors in the screen beside the high altar. He stood on the highest step, facing the altar, with a lighted torch in his left hand. As soon as the lesson was over, he turned towards the clergy in the choir and sang the words '*Hodie natus celorum rex de virgine nasci dignatus est*' (The king of heaven consented on this day to be born for us of a virgin). At *celorum rex* he raised his right

72

hand towards heaven, at *de virgine* he extended it to the statue of the Virgin beside the altar, and at *dignatus est* he genuflected. The clergy replied: *'Ut hominem perditum ad celestia regna revocaret'* (That he should call home outcast man to the kingdom of heaven). Next, three boys from the south side of the choir and three from the north, all dressed like the first, came to the lowest step of the altar. The first boy descended to join them, and all seven faced the clergy, singing the *Gloria in excelsis deo:* 'Glory to God on high and on earth peace, goodwill towards men.' When this was over, the boys walked through the middle of the choir and out through the door beneath the screen. They were to walk, said Grandisson, *'morose'*, which means 'slowly' or 'soberly'; the excitement of the occasion must sometimes have caused a headlong rush![2]

Matins was followed by the Christmas midnight mass, with the precentor or the dean as celebrant; the chief members of the chapter were expected to take the leading parts in the services on the great festivals. Altogether, three masses were said in the choir on Christmas Day, another unique occurrence. The second was celebrated by the chancellor after lauds, in the early hours of the morning, while it was still dark. The third was the high mass in the middle of the morning, at which the bishop officiated if he were present, if not, the cleric next in seniority.[3] These Christmas services must have been impressive. The bells were rung at greater length than usual and the inside of the cathedral was bright with extra lights: seven on the high altar, three before the cross, and others around the ambulatories.[4] With all the additional prayers and ceremonies, it was a long haul from vespers on Christmas Eve to high mass on Christmas Day, with little opportunity for rest. No doubt the clergy were glad to get off to their dinners when high mass was over, the canons to their own houses and the vicars, secondaries and choristers probably accompanying their respective canons. The feasting on Christmas Day was private and individual, however, and is consequently not mentioned in the records. But three days later, on 28 December, there was a festival about which we know more: the Feast of the Holy Innocents. This day was widely observed in medieval churches as a holiday from the normal routine, involving what is nowadays referred to as 'role-reversal'. The junior members of the cathedral clergy – the choristers – changed places with the seniors for the day. One of the choristers was chosen as boy bishop to impersonate the real bishop and to lead the services, while the others took the place of the canons. All the clergy were involved and the activities spread from the cathedral into the Close and even into the city.

The ceremonies of 28 December began at vespers on the previous day, the Feast of St John the Evangelist. The boy bishop, representing, in Grandisson's words, 'Christ the child, true and eternal' and kitted out with a miniature mitre, gloves and pastoral staff,[5] came to the steps of the high altar accompanied by the rest of the choristers, all dressed in silk copes. There he sang a text based on the Book of Revelation (Chapter 14) which was chosen as a reminder of the children slaughtered by King Herod: *'Centum quadraginta quatuor milia qui empti de terra...'* (The hundred and forty-four thousand which were redeemed from the earth....They reign with God, and the Lamb of God with them.). After this, the boy bishop processed through the choir towards the screen. He offered incense to the cross above the screen, his entourage sang chants and prayers, and he delivered a blessing, first to the clergy in the choir and then to the laity in the nave. When the blessing was over, he returned to the choir and sat in a special seat. After vespers he led the clergy in the service of compline.

Grandisson's Ordinal, which sets out all the information about the events of the eve of the festival, is less forthcoming about what happened on the day itself. This was a sensitive matter, since the Feast of the Innocents was often marked by wild disorder. Not only the choristers but the adult clergy were apt to join in scenes of mockery and horseplay, in ways that would seem strange and shocking to us now. In 1360 Grandisson solemnly warned the cathedral clergy against 'inept and harmful games, indecent to clerical honesty' to which they might be tempted during the Christmas season.[6] We have to remember that the cathedral was their place of work for 365 days of the year and this was the one day when the rules did not apply – like the last day of work before Christmas in an office or a factory. The clergy, like modern employees, could easily overstep the mark, and the bishop did not wish to encourage them in that direction. So the Ordinal merely laid down that the boy bishop should administer a second blessing to the laity at lauds on 28 December and a third at vespers in the evening, after which his office was to come to an end. The boys were to withdraw from the choir during vespers and go straight off to bed in their dormitory.[7]

Fortunately, we are able to supplement this account of the boy-bishop celebrations from a set of regulations which were drawn up, in the fifteenth or early sixteenth century, in another attempt to keep the festivities under control. Normally during the year, the choristers left the choir after prime and had breakfast, like all their other meals, in the houses of their canons. On 28 December, however, the boy bishop's canon had to give all the boys a special breakfast in a room called 'the bishop's chamber'. Either breakfast had become too lavish or the boys expected it to be, since the regulations laid down that in future the food should be simple: a pennyworth of bread, two quarts of ale, two or three pennyworth of meat or a pennyworth of butter or cheese – total cost not more than 4d. or 6d. When breakfast was over, the bishop and his companions went in procession through the city to St Nicholas's Priory, no doubt because St Nicholas was the patron saint of choristers and schoolboys (in many towns the boy-bishop ceremonies actually took place on 6 December, the Feast of St Nicholas). Later on the clergy presented gifts of gloves to important people in the city, and money was collected, some of which became the boy bishop's personal property. (Much the same use to happen, until as recently as 1844, in the famous Montem ceremony at Eton College.)[8] At midday, the boy bishop was treated by his canon to a good dinner, to which he could invite up to six of his friends, though he had to pay 4d. a head for their food from his profits if the canon asked him to. In the afternoon, all the boys went back to the choir for vespers, at which point the celebrations were supposed to come to an end, but not surprisingly the boys and some of the adults tried to prolong them further. Apparently the boys had sometimes been involved in the 'bearing of wine and a torch' to the college of the vicars in Kalendarhay, where some kind of clerical stag-party went on, and some canons used to provide a second special breakfast on 29 December. Those who drew up the regulations were determined, like Grandisson, that the feast should end strictly at vespers on the 28th and both these extra practices were banned.[9]

The six and a half weeks from Ash Wednesday to Easter Sunday were marked by a series of important days with special observances. We do not know how the cathedral community celebrated Shrove Tuesday, but it probably followed customs in use elsewhere. Schoolboys took cocks to school to fight them (perhaps the choristers did so too) and everyone who could had a special dinner with pancakes to use up their eggs. Shrove Tuesday was the last day of self-indulgence before a long period of austerity. From Ash Wednesday until the day before Easter the cathedral took on a plainer appearance. The images and crosses were all veiled, and the altar frontals and vestments were of purple, as they had been since Septuagesima. Daily life was also plainer, since everybody – clergy and laity – had to abstain from certain foods. No red meat might be eaten, no poultry and no white meat; this included eggs, milk, butter and cheese. The only animal food permitted was fish. In church, the services were directed towards humility, repentance and doing penance.

On Ash Wednesday many of the laity attended high mass in the cathedral. Before mass a sermon was preached 'to the people', no doubt of a severe nature, castigating the sins of the age and calling on sinners to repent. Next came the distribution of ashes. The clergy, and perhaps the laity, came forward one by one, and each had ashes smeared on the forehead in the form of a cross, while the officiating priest declared in Latin: 'Remember man that thou art ashes, and to ashes shalt thou return'. Then there was a procession to the doors of the church (probably the west doors), consisting of the clergy and the 'penitents', who were presumably pious people or people ordered by their confessors to attend. The penitents were expelled from the doors, as a warning of the fate of sinners, and the doors were shut behind them.[10]

There were two or three days of relaxation from these hardships. The fourth Sunday in Lent (now known as Mothering Sunday) was a day of some festivity and the clergy were allowed to wear vestments of gold and purple mixed, instead of purple alone.[11] Palm Sunday saw the first of the great processions of spring, in the open air; we shall return to this presently. Maundy Thursday in particular was set aside for charity to others. The word 'maundy' comes from Christ's commandment (*mandatum*) to his disciples on the first Maundy Thursday that they should 'love one another; as I have loved you, so you are to love one another ... ' (John 13:34 – 5). He showed his love for them by washing their feet. Accordingly, before high mass, the clergy set off in procession to the doors, this time to reconcile the penitents standing outside and to receive them back into the bosom of the Church. At the mass, the officiating priest consecrated three wafers of bread instead of one, and put two aside for the following day. When mass was over, there was dinner, and after dinner the high altar and all the other altars were stripped of their coverings and ceremonially washed by the clergy with wine and water. After the washing, the clergy assembled in the chapter house. They listened to the reading of the Passion of St John, a sermon was preached and two of the clergy washed the feet of the others, while the choir sang psalms and antiphons.[12] It was a widespread custom in the Middle Ages for the rich to give alms to the poor on Maundy Thursday – a custom which survives today in the Maundy money ceremony – and this also happened at the cathedral. From 1308 there are references in the accounts to the feeding of sixty poor people, each of them receiving a farthingsworth of bread, a halfpennyworth of drink and relishes and a penny in ready money. Later in the fourteenth century the drink was omitted – perhaps it was thought unsuitable on such a solemn day – and the poor were given an extra halfpenny instead.[13]

Lent reached its climax on Good Friday. The images and crosses were still veiled, and the altars were now bare of their coverings. The clergy attended the services barefoot, and the services (except for matins, lauds and high mass) were said 'privately', in an undertone, rather than being audibly performed. Early in the morning, the Easter sepulchre was set up on the north side of the high altar. At Exeter this was a moveable structure consisting of some kind of tall cupboard with a door, no doubt in a Gothic style with pinnacles, not unlike a smaller version of the bishop's throne, perhaps. Towards the end of the morning, after nones and before high mass, a large portable crucifix was carried in by two priests and placed in front of the high altar. The clergy, still barefoot 'in memory of the wounded feet of the Crucified', approached the cross in turn to adore it, seniors first. This was the ceremony known as 'creeping to the cross', which was generally done by crawling on hands and knees across the floor in order to express the greatest possible degree of humility and sorrow. When the clergy had all adored the cross, it was carried by the two priests to one of the lesser altars in the church, so that the laity might adore it in the same way. Mass was then celebrated in the choir, but instead of a new wafer being consecrated, one of the two reserved from the day before was used. Vespers followed immediately after mass. Then, in a final ceremony, the portable crucifix was placed inside the sepulchre together with the third of the consecrated wafers, to represent the placing of Christ's body in the tomb. The sepulchre was censed with incense and the door was closed; all knelt, adored the sepulchre, and withdrew.[14]

On Holy Saturday, the cathedral began to be prepared for Easter. The altars were dressed again, though the images and crosses remained veiled for most of the day. During the morning, before high mass, all the lights in the church were put out. Then, carrying unlit candles, the clergy processed down the south aisle of the nave to the vicinity of the font. There 'new fire' was kindled, probably with flint and tinder, and a few drops of holy water were sprinkled on it in blessing. One of the clergy lit a taper on a long staff and when the procession returned to the choir, this taper was used to light the Paschal or Easter candle, a very large candle in a special tall candlestick on the north side of the altar. Other lights in the church were also lit. Later, the procession returned to the font, which had been emptied and filled with fresh water, and this too was blessed. Finally, after compline in the evening, the coverings were removed from the images and crosses.[15] The church was now ready for Easter.

On Sunday morning all the clergy came to the choir at dawn in order to re-enact the first visit of the disciples to the sepulchre. First, they lit all the lights in the church (as they did on Christmas Day) to make the place as bright as possible. Then they went to the sepulchre, led by their seniors, took out the consecrated wafer and placed it on the high altar. The two seniors took the portable crucifix in their arms and led the others in procession out of the north door of the choir and in again by the south door, singing the great words of the Epistle to the Romans, 'Christus Resurgens'. 'Christ being raised from the dead dieth no more; death hath no more dominion over him. For in that he liveth he liveth unto God. Alleluia! Alleluia!' As they pronounced these words, the bells of the cathedral rang out to signify the Resurrection. The crucifix was placed by the high altar as a visible sign of the fact, and as the clergy placed it there they cried 'Surrexit dominus de sepulcro' (the Lord has risen from the tomb!).[16]

The joyful season of Easter ushered in the spring, the time of the great processions. Small processions, as we have seen, took place inside the cathedral every day, but in the spring the clergy everywhere went on more lengthy journeys, leaving the shelter of their churches to perambulate the countryside and the cities. There were seven great processional days: Palm Sunday, the four Rogation days (25 April and the Monday, Tuesday and Wednesday before Ascension Day), Ascension Day itself and Corpus Christi, which falls three weeks later, on the Thursday after Trinity Sunday.[17] The first six of these days were ancient festivals that had been held in England ever since the Anglo-Saxon period. The feast of Corpus Christi grew up in the thirteenth century in honour of the Eucharist or mass, reflecting the more frequent celebration of masses in churches which we discussed in Chapter 2. The feast was ordered to be held in all churches by the Council of Vienne in 1311, and came to be observed in England soon afterwards. Three of the days – Palm Sunday, Ascension Day and Corpus Christi – were festal or joyous occasions, which centred on the singing of hymns in praise of Christ the King, Christ the Ascended and Christ in the Eucharist. The other four, the Rogation days, were days of penitence and 'asking', which is what Rogation means – the 'Major Rogation', which also came to be designated as St Mark's Day – was a Christian substitution for the pagan festival of Robigalia, on which the Romans made processions and prayers for the success of the growing crops. The days before Ascension – the 'Minor Rogations' – were instituted by St Mametius in southern France in about 470, to pray for deliverance from earthquakes. Fasting was observed on all the Rogation days and the processions centred on the saying of the litany, with prayers offered to the saints, by name, for their intercession, and prayers to God for peace, prosperity and plenty of crops.

The great processions formed up in the cathedral during the morning. Those on Palm Sunday, Ascension Day and Corpus Christi did not go as far or take as long as the Rogation ones, and they set off at about nine o'clock, before the high mass of the day.[18] As well as the cathedral clergy, various other people also took part. We hear at different times of the monks of St Nicholas's Priory, the rectors and chaplains of the city churches, the mayor and citizens, and the city guild of skinners taking part in processions.[19] In 1470 even the king and his household joined the Palm Sunday procession.[20] The clergy went out of the cathedral through the west door or via the cloisters, down Palace Gate or Bear Street into South Street, and along the High Street.[21] In 1322 Bishop Stapledon talks of the Palm Sunday and Corpus Christi processions going out of the East Gate, from which they may have retraced their steps down the High Street or come round Southernhay and into the Close via the South Gate.[22]

The Rogation processions were longer and more ambitious. They began after high mass at the end of the morning.[23] First came a dragon carried on a pole; next, a banner displaying a lion; third, the other church banners; fourth, the cross; fifth, the clergy, and (probably) sixth, the laity. The route led to another church in the city or the nearby suburbs. Here the procession stopped to celebrate a 'fasting mass', so called because no midday meal was eaten, before returning in the afternoon. On Rogation Wednesday and Ascension Day the dragon was demoted from the head of the procession and put behind the lion and the other banners. According to *The Golden Legend*, the great medieval book about festivals and saints' days, the dragon represented the devil and Rogation Monday and Tuesday stood for the first and second eras of the world, in which the devil triumphed: before the Law of Moses and under the Law. Rogation Wednesday denoted the third era, in which the devil was cast down by Christ, so on that day the dragon was deposed from his pre-eminent position.[24]

Walking about in the open air, singing and praying and carrying banners, is hungry work, especially when there is no midday meal. On Rogation days it seems to have been the custom for the clergy to partake of some refreshment when their work was done. Thus the London diarist Henry Machyn, describing the Rogation processions in the middle of the sixteenth century, says that the clergy had 'good cheer' when everything was over, and the records of parish churches often allude to the purchase of food and drink on these days.[25] So it was at the cathedral; the accounts between 1386 and 1403 mention an annual expenditure of between 22s. and 48s. on what is called in Latin *custus flauonum*, 'the cost of the flans'.[26] These flans were eaten on Rogation Days. They were made of pastry and filled with a mixture of eggs, cheese, butter and cream, flavoured with pepper, saffron and honey. No doubt they were produced by the canons' baker, who made the canons' daily allowance of loaves, and the large scale of the ingredients shows that there were plenty of them. Anything from 3 to 7½ bushels of flour were used, 5 to 10 shillingsworth of cheese, and 2 or 3 pounds of pepper. The number of eggs was never less than 1500 and usually reached 2400; on one occasion it rose to 3450!

It is amusing to compare the prices of the ingredients in the late fourteenth century with those of today: eggs, 5d. to 6d. a hundred; flour or dough, 8d. to 1s. 6d. a bushel; honey 1s. 4d. a gallon; pepper, 1s. to 2s. a pound, and saffron, 4d. to 8d. an ounce. Prices in those days varied from year to year depending on the harvest or, in the case of pepper, on the state of the overseas trade. Pepper was brought from the East and the usual price appears to have been 1s. 1d. a pound, but in the early 1390s it soared for a time to 2s. Eggs were generally sold at 5d. a hundred and the cathedral seems to have resented paying more; when prices rose to 6d., efforts were made to buy at least some of the requirements at 5d.

There are recipes for flans in fifteenth-century cookery books which show

Order of Rogationtide Processions

A plan of the head of the processions for Rogation Wednesday and Ascension Day: 1. Lion Banner 2. Other banners 3. Dragon 4. Holy sacrament in a shrine 5. Incense. The 'doughnuts' are the tonsured heads of the clergy who carried them.

that they were made in much the same way then as they are today, excep
that the use of deep stone ovens meant that the pastry-cases were mos
easily filled inside the oven, using a scoop with a long handle.

Take milk and yolks of eggs, and draw it through a strainer with whit
sugar, or black sugar, and melt fair butter and put thereto, and salt. Anc
make fair coffins, and set them in the oven till they be hard. Then take
peel with a dish on the end and fill the dish with the mixture, and pou.
into the coffins, and let bake a little while; then take them out into a fai.
dish and cast white sugar thereon, and serve forth. [27]

This is a recipe for a sweet flan, but the Exeter Rogationtide flans wer
evidently semi-sweet, as they were flavoured with pepper and honey, anc
must have resembled certain modern cheesecakes. The word 'coffin', whicl
also appears in Latin in the cathedral accounts, is an incongruous word t
find in a cookery book. But originally it meant a basket or simila
receptacle, and was the name given to what we call a pastry-case, untaintec
by its modern funereal associations.

One other great festivity was held in the second half of the fifteentl
century, on 28 June. This was the day before the Feast of St Peter and S
Paul which, from at least the early twelfth century, was the cathedral'
patronal festival. [28] The secular part of the celebrations centred on a bonfir
on the cathedral green – hardly a practice that would be allowed today
Even in those days it was questionable, since most of the green consisted o
the burial ground and the dean and chapter normally prohibited secula
activities in the area. However, the lighting of bonfires round abou
Midsummer Day (24 June) was a very ancient custom in England anc
perhaps it was thought to be appropriate on this occasion as an honour t
the church's patron saints. The money for the bonfire was raised by takin
a collection among the canons, any deficit being made up out of the fabri
fund. In 1450, when we first hear of the practice, the faggots for the bonfir
cost 4s. 2d.; the canons contributed 3s. 8d. and the fabric fund 6d. [29] In th
following year, as well as a bonfire, there were payments for '205 shield
made of paper, with the keys of Peter and the sword of Paul, for deliverin
to the *famulis* [servants of the canons to ride on the vigil of St Peter'
The cost of the paper was 8d., and the shields were painted at three (late.
four) for a penny. The number of canons' servants was probably onl
between 100 and 150, so other people must have taken part; perhaps th
vicars choral and the choristers, who were also attached to the canons
households, joined in the fun as well. Unfortunately, the fabric accounts d
not explain the form of the 'riding'. It may have been a procession, since i
is once referred to as a 'walking', or it may have been a battle between tw
mounted armies: Decani v. Cantoris, or Peter v. Paul. The shields appear t
have been rather small, judging from the modest amount of paper used, s
perhaps they acted as badges of identity.

For a few years, the activities on St Peter's Eve were evidently ver
popular. In 1452, 160 shields were paid for, in 1453, 180, in 1455, 205, i
1456, 210, and in 1460, 168. In 1455 a new activity is mentioned: 'an abbo
and others playing an interlude in the cemetery' (an interlude being a dram
or play). The abbot must have been a mock abbot or 'abbot of misrule'

accompanied by his retinue; abbots were considered fair game for parody. A century earlier, Grandisson had taken exception to the antics of a certain 'abbot of Brothelyngham' and his followers, who acted irreverent scenes in the city dressed as monks.[30] A hundred years later, in 1559, when there were still a few abbeys in England, Queen Elizabeth I was entertained at Epiphany by revellers dressed as abbots with wolves' heads![31] The climax of the Exeter revels, as far as the fabric rolls are concerned, took place in 1461, when 240 shields were paid for. After that, the jollifications seem to have declined. There are no records of canons' donations after 1460, and the shields are mentioned for the last time in the rolls for the following year, though the fire was still being paid for in 1505 and possibly later. What a picture it must have made: the men and boys on horseback with their badges, the shouts and cries, and the flare and crackle of the bonfire as night came on. The smoke and noise seem almost to reach us across the centuries, as they once drifted across the rooftops on a summer evening to the people of Exeter.

9

The Saints

We suggested in Chapter 3 that a medieval church was a kind of model of the whole Church, and particularly of the Church Triumphant in heaven. Enthroned in the centre were images of Christ. As you walked up the nave in a cathedral or an ordinary parish church, the image which dominated your view was the cross or 'rood' above the choir-screen. Upon the cross hung the crucified figure of Christ and a little below it were statues of the Virgin Mary and St John. If you looked through the choir-screen into the choir, you saw another, smaller cross on the high altar. Over the altar was a canopy, shading the box which contained the body of Christ in the form of consecrated bread, the holiest object in the church. Christ's was the chief presence in both the choir and the nave, and round about him, like the courtiers of a medieval king, were images of his mother, the angels and the saints, carved, painted and embroidered on wood, stone, glass and cloth.

Christians have always regarded Christ as a king, and the people of the Middle Ages naturally imagined him to be like the kings of their own day. Medieval kings were important figures whom ordinary folk could rarely approach directly. If you wanted to escape their anger or ask them to do you a favour, it was wise to approach an intermediary – a royal servant or a courtier – who could negotiate on your behalf. Likewise, in the kingdom of heaven you asked Christ's servants – the angels and the saints – to intercede with him. All churches, therefore, had subsidiary cults of the saints as well as the central cult of Christ. People came to church to honour the saints as well as God, and prayed to God through them as well as directly. There are many reminders of this fact in Exeter cathedral today, from the chapels and altars dedicated to saints to the carvings and paintings of them on the walls and the windows, and there used to be even more of them. But the saints were not present in the cathedral only symbolically, in paintings or as statues. Many of them were also there in a bodily sense, represented by their bones or their clothing. In the early centuries of the Church, until about 1200 or 1300, it was essential for churches to possess such relics because most people found it easier to relate to Christianity through tangible objects than in purely abstract terms. Saints' bones and clothes, it was believed, retained the holiness of their owners and could transmit this holiness, through touch and sight, to other people.

Accordingly, when Athelstan refounded the abbey at Exeter which later became the cathedral, he gave it not only material wealth, in the form of lands, but a spiritual endowment, in the form of relics. The abbey and the cathedral owed their subsequent prestige to the relics quite as much as to the lands. We possess three inventories of the relics, drawn up in the late eleventh and twelfth centuries. They purport to be lists of Athelstan's gifts, but in fact some of the relics recorded are later acquisitions; for example, those relating to St Edward the Martyr, who died in 978, long after Athelstan.[1] Nevertheless, the final collection was impressive, boasting relics of Christ, his mother and the Apostles as well as more recent saints. There was part of the manger of the stable in Bethlehem, some water from the River Jordan – to commemorate Christ's baptism – and stones from the mountain where he fasted. There were fragments of the wood of the cross and of the sword and lance with which his body was pierced, drops of his blood and part of a candle which the angel allegedly lit in the sepulchre. The other relics included some of the Virgin Mary's hair, bits of her clothes and her pillow, parts of the beard, hair and clothing of St Peter, a piece of St Paul's neck, the finger of St Mary Magdalene, four of St Agatha's teeth and part of her veil. There were bones or belongings of both St Johns, St Andrew (his staff), St James, St Stephen (part of his head, some blood and a few of the stones with which he was killed) and some of the coals on which St Lawrence was roasted. There were also other relics, mostly unspecified, of nearly a hundred other holy men and women: early Roman martyrs, saintly French bishops and saints of the South West of England like St Petrock, St Sidwell and St Winwaloe.

The relic collection made the cathedral by far the most important church, in terms of possessions of spiritual significance, in the whole of Devon and Cornwall. People flocked to the cathedral to pray at the relics, particularly for their injuries to be healed and their diseases cured, and an account of about 1125 informs us that miracles took place. A deaf and dumb woman received the faculties of hearing and speech, a man who arrived there a cripple walked away, and a woman whose arms had withered was able to clap her hands.[2] The relics were added to by Bishop Briwere, who donated hairs of Christ and St Peter, relics of St Stephen and St Demetrius, and some 'oil of St Katherine', which he may have acquired on his pilgrimage to the Holy Land in 1227. Later still, in the early fourteenth century, Dean Bartholomew of St Lawrence (d. 1326) contributed some of the bones of St Brannoc of Braunton.[3]

Like other great churches the cathedral held an annual festival in honour of the relics, in this case on the Monday after Ascension Day, and they were also shown to the public on other major festivals. One of the clergy seems to have been allotted the task of explaining what the relics were, and encouraging people to offer money to them. Between 1386 and 1388 Thomas Abbot, one of the annuellars, was given a gallon of wine a year (price 8d.) for 'proclaiming the relics'; this must have been thirsty work![4] The people, for their part, responded. The records show that during the fourteenth century sums of money, usually between 5s. and £1, were given to the relics during Lent, on Good Friday, at Whitsuntide and on Corpus Christi.[5] We hear very little of the relics after 1400, but some of them were still exhibited in 1506 in the Lady chapel. They included a thorn from the crown of Our Lord, part of the cross and relics of various saints enclosed or mounted in silver crosses or reliquaries, some of them ornamented with precious stones.[6]

Besides the relics, there were special chapels and altars dedicated to certain saints, at which their devotees could pray. By the fourteenth century the cathedral itself was considered to be dedicated to the Virgin Mary, St Peter and St Paul. The original dedication was actually to Mary and St Peter alone. It is first mentioned in connection with the Saxon monastery in the tenth century and subsequently passed to the cathedral.[7] The dedication to St Paul appears to have been added much later, during the thirteenth century, perhaps because it was customary to hold the cathedral's dedication feast on 29 June (St Peter and St Paul), rather than on one of the other feast-days dedicated to St Peter alone.[8] At all events, when Bishop Grandisson dedicated the new high altar of the cathedral in 1328, he did so in the names of the Virgin Mary, St Peter and St Paul, and St Paul's statue was duly placed next to those of the other saints beside the high altar.[9] We do not know what altars and chapels, apart from the high altar, were to be found in the first Saxon cathedral, but the arrangements are little clearer with regard to the second, Norman foundation. It appears that by the second half of the thirteenth century the Norman cathedral possessed a Lady chapel (first mentioned in 1236) and at least six other altars. These, in order of their appearance in records, were the altars of the Holy Cross (1224–8), St Edmund the King (1263), St John the Baptist with St Blaise and St Piran (1271), St Mary (1272–7), St Richard with St Radegund (1284) and St Paul (1285).[10] Popular devotion to most of these saints was widespread in medieval times and only two need comment: St Piran, who was from Cornwall, and St Richard, presumably Richard, Bishop of Chichester, who died in 1253 and was canonized in 1276. St Richard's name may have been added to an earlier altar of St Radegund.

The new cathedral that was built after 1270 was larger than its predecessors and contained more chapels and altars. At the east end two new chapels were constructed beside the Lady chapel. In the records for the 1280s they are referred to as having been recently built, and at first they were not dedicated to any specific saints, so they were not replacements for earlier chapels.[11] Their dedications – the chapel on the north side to St John the Evangelist and the one the south side to St Gabriel – must therefore have also been new. The dedication to St Gabriel was evidently suggested by Bishop Branscombe, who had a particular devotion to the archangel and built a chapel in his honour at Bishop's Court.[12] The choice was an appropriate one for the site, as was that of St John, for the archangel appeared to the Virgin at the Annunciation and St John was with her at the Crucifixion.[13]

Moving westwards from the east end, the two small altars in the choir beside the high altar were dedicated to martyrs: English archbishops on the north side (St Thomas Becket and St Alphege) and early Christian deacons on the south (St Stephen and St Lawrence).[14] The two double chapels half-way down the choir-aisles were dedicated to St Andrew and St Katherine (north side) and St Mary Magdalene and St James (south side).[15] There are no records of these chapels and dedications dating from before the building of the new cathedral, and they were probably new to it. They may have been suggested by the cathedral's relics, which included items linked with all four saints, and they have a satisfying symmetry, since the festivals of St Andrew and St Katherine occur together in November, and those of St Mary Magdalene and St James in July. It is not certain which of the altars in each chapel were dedicated to which saint, but as it is polite for a gentleman to walk on the outside of the pavement, nearer the road, when escorting a lady, it accords with etiquette if not with history to place the ladies on the inside.

When the nave was rebuilt, most of the altars and chapels established there were survivors from the old cathedral. The altars of the Holy Cross, St Edmund and St Mary continued to occupy positions similar to their previous ones, while the altars of St Paul and St John the Baptist were moved into new chapels opening off the north and south towers respectively. There were, however, one or two changes. The altar next to St Mary in front of the choir-screen (originally the altar of St John the Baptist) was rededicated to St Nicholas,[16] and the altar of St Richard and St Radegund disappeared.[17] Nor do we hear after 1271 of St Blaise or St Piran, who had previously had a share in the altar of St John the Baptist.

When Grandisson became Bishop of Exeter in 1327, he interested himself in the worship of the saints, to a greater extent then most of his predecessors. Grandisson had spent a good deal of his life in France. He had studied theology in Paris and had been a chaplain and personal friend of Pope John XXII, who had appointed him bishop. He was consequently well up in the latest fashions of worship in continental Europe and Exeter must have struck him as rather old-fashioned and provincial in its manner of worship. Indeed, he encountered the fact on arrival, for when he came to be enthroned in the cathedral on 22 August 1328, in the 'octave' or week after the feast of the Virgin Mary's Assumption, he found that the octave was being observed in a modest fashion, without the processions and music he was used to.[18] Accordingly, he set out to make changes, not interfering with the dedications of the chapels and altars, but seeking to rationalize and improve the worship of the saints in the daily services. In 1333 he ordered the cathedral to celebrate the nativity of St John the Baptist on 24 June as a 'medium double' or feast of the second rank: hitherto, contrary to the custom of other churches, it had been only a simple feast of the fifth rank.[19] In 1338 he 'appropriated' (transferred the revenues of) the church of St Merryn in Cornwall to the cathedral to finance the celebration of the Octave of the Assumption as a major double (first-rank feast) and the translations of St Edward the Confessor (13 October) and St Thomas Becket (7 July) as medium doubles.[20] Later in 1343, he got the pope to issue an indulgence for all who performed or attended the feasts of the Virgin Mary and St Edward in the cathedral.[21] Grandisson wished to increase the honour done to these saints, one imagines, because Mary was by now the most popular saint throughout the Catholic Church, while Edward and Thomas were the most popular in England. Up to the fourteenth century, Edward the Confessor was the chief patron saint of the English royal family and hence effectively the patron saint of England. Moreover, he had a special link with Exeter, since he had sanctioned the foundation of the cathedral in 1050 and had personally attended the enthronement of the first bishop.

In 1337 Grandisson issued his Ordinal (mentioned in Chapter 7), which prescribes how the daily services were to be performed in the cathedral. The Ordinal reveals that by this time, over half the days of the year (about 187) were given up to the feasts of saints or to the octaves which followed them. The saints in the Exeter calendar were those whom one would have expected to find commemorated anywhere in England: the Virgin, the Apostles, the Roman martyrs, several French saints popular with the Norman conquerors, the chief Anglo-Saxon saints and a handful of English saints who had been canonized since the Conquest. The only Exeter saints who were not widely recognized elsewhere were St Brannoc, whose relics were in the cathedral, and St David, St Kerrian, St Petrock and St Sidwell, all of whom had churches dedicated to them in the city. Grandisson tolerated the celebration of these local saints; indeed, he was probably responsible for writing up the legends of St Sidwell into a form suitable for reading at matins on her day (2 August).[22] Grandisson seems to have hoped that more of the major saints would be honoured with altars in the cathedral. In his directions for the festivals of five of them – St Edmund of Abingdon, St Edward the Confessor, St Margaret, St Martin and St Michael – he provided for processions to be made to the appropriate altars if they existed.[23] This was a feasible plan in 1337, when the cathedral was still being built and when there were plenty of clergy available to serve new altars as chantry priests or vicars choral. At the end of the 1340s, however, the Black Death put an end to this situation. The number of clergy fell and for the next thirty years there were too few to look after the existing altars in the cathedral, let alone new ones.

We can see from all this that the fortunes of the saints on earth are erratic compared with their serenity in heaven. There are fashions in saints, like everything else, and as some rise in prominence (like the Virgin Mary, St Edward and St Thomas Becket), others are neglected. We have examples of this at Exeter in the disappearance of the altars of St Richard and St Radegund, St Blaise and St Piran. The process of change continued during and after Grandisson's time. We noted in Chapter 3 that the chapel of St Edmund the King at the west end of the cathedral probably fell into disuse after the Black Death, while the chapel of St Mary Magdalene and St James was turned into a vestry during the fifteenth century.[24] Their places were filled by other saints, notably St Anne and St Michael, who were given more prominence.

The cult of St Anne became increasingly popular in the fourteenth century, partly reflecting a greater awareness of family life, for the legends of St Anne centre upon her role as the mother and bringer-up of the Virgin Mary. There is still an original sculpture on the screen of the Speke chantry showing St Anne teaching the Virgin to read. Grandisson introduced her cult to Exeter in 1352, and the cathedral possesses a fragment of the mass for her day (26 July), marked with his handwriting.[25] Later, in 1381, Pope Urban VI instructed all the English bishops, including the Bishop of Exeter, to see that St Anne's Day was observed in their churches.[26] This was obeyed, and her feast day came to be celebrated in the cathedral as a

St Anne and the Virgin
*The introduction of the cult of St Anne, the mother of the Virgin,
symbolized a growing interest in family life. Here, on the early Tudor
screen of the Speke chantry, St Anne teaches the Virgin to read, as a
contemporary mother might have done.*

feast of the fifth grade, with nine lessons.[27] The cult of St Michael seems to have grown in importance at the very end of the century. The first recorded reference to an image of St Michael in the south transept dates from 1398, when Canon John Michel was buried beside it. By 1410 a portable altar and collecting box had been established in the same area.[28] There is a mention of money being put into the box, perhaps by visitors from Cornwall, for St Michael was a popular saint with the Cornish and his statue filled the gap left by the disappearance of the cult of St Piran.

There were further attempts to develop cults of saints in the 1420s. In 1425 Bishop Lacy granted an indulgence to people who visited the altars of St Agatha, St Anne, St Katherine and St Mary Magdalene.[29] Since all these saints were women, it rather looks as if the aim was to encourage women to visit the cathedral by giving them altars at which they might like to pray. The altars of St Anne and St Agatha were new ones and reflected, in St Anne's case, a rising popularity, while St Agatha was probably chosen because her veil and teeth were among the cathedral's relics. We do not know where these altars were sited, but it seems likely that they were existing altars which did not already have dedications, such as the altar in the Grandisson chapel and the one by the tomb of the Earl of Devon. No further mention of the altars of St Anne and St Agatha was ever made, and since the altar of St Mary Magdalene later disappeared, it seems that this particular attempt to stir up popular devotion was not successful.

The cult of St Bertin, a French abbot who died in 698, was more long-lived. The fabric rolls mention the existence of a lamp of St Bertin for the first time in 1424 and an altar dedicated to him was recorded in 1431.[30] The references make it clear that both were identical with the altar of St Mary below the choir-screen, which was usually known as the 'Bratton' or 'Barton' altar. The cult of St Bertin probably developed from a misunderstanding of this name. An amateur historian may have thought that 'Barton' should really be 'Bertin', or someone who found out about St Bertin in France (perhaps while taking part in the Hundred Years War) may have decided that the Bratton altar would be an appropriate focal point for a cult of the saint in the cathedral. Whatever the reason, the altar of St Mary continued to be referred to as the altar of St Bertin until 1466, after which St Bertin was either forgotten or his sainthood disproved, and the references are once again to the Bratton or Barton altar.[31]

One cannot help suspecting that Bishop Lacy had a hand in originating these new cults of the 1420s: he certainly helped to popularize those of St Anne and St Agatha. Grandisson excepted, Lacy was the bishop who seems to have taken most interest in the worship and the cults of saints at Exeter Cathedral. In 1428 he arranged that the choristers should sing an antiphon in the cathedral each day in honour of the Virgin,[32] and in 1443 he started an entirely new cult in honour of St Raphael.[33] Raphael, whose name means 'God has healed', is one of the three archangels and the hero of the Book of Tobit in the Apocrypha. This tells how Raphael healed the pious Jewish father Tobit from blindness and freed his son and daughter-in-law from the attentions of a demon. The story was well known to the Exeter clergy because the Book of Tobit was read at cathedral matins each September, but unlike his fellow archangels, Gabriel and Michael, Raphael did not have a cult of his own anywhere in England, it seems, until Lacy decided to remedy the lack in 1443. By this time Lacy was in his mid-seventies and had been infirm for several years so he had a personal interest in healing. In 1443 he drew up services for a Feast of St Raphael to be held on 5 October, exactly one week after St Michael's Day. The services were submitted to the pope for his approval, and were examined and duly sanctioned on the pope's behalf by the Chancellor of Oxford University. Lacy then authorized the feast to be celebrated at the cathedral and throughout the diocese. He also tried to get it established at some other major cathedrals: Hereford, Salisbury and York. The feast was first observed at Exeter as a minor double (third rank), but in 1499 Bishop Redmayn promoted it one rank higher, to medium double, at the request of the dean and chapter. It seems to have been kept at Exeter and Hereford down to the Reformation, but never became very popular in other parts of the country.

The cult of St Raphael was almost the last important saint-cult to be introduced in the cathedral. The last of all was established by Sir John Speke, a West Country knight, when he dedicated his new chantry chapel in the north choir-aisle to St George in 1518.[34] In the middle of the fourteenth century St George had begun to replace St Edward the Confessor as the patron saint of the royal family and of England. The Order of the Garter was founded in his honour in 1348 and he was thought to have helped the English at the battle of Agincourt. He was also regarded as 'Our Lady's knight', her special soldier, which explains the placing of his chapel close to hers and the presence of her statues on its screen.[35]

By 1518, however, new-saint cults were becoming unusual. During the fifteenth century, fashions in worship had taken fresh directions. People were becoming interested not only in saints but in the direct worship of God. Of course, there had always been devotion to God Himself and the cathedral had possessed an altar in honour of the Cross ever since the 1220s.[36] In 1379, when Bishop Brantingham set up his chantry and altar in the nave he caused it to be dedicated to the Trinity, not to a saint.[37] This kind of devotion developed still further in the fifteenth century. A cult of the Name of Jesus became popular. Masses called 'Jesus masses' were celebrated in honour of the Name, an annual feast was established on 7 August to commemorate it and chapels were dedicated to it, as Jesus College, Cambridge, survives to remind us. The cult of the Name of Jesus spread to Exeter – we find Jesus masses being endowed in the churches of St George, St Mary Arches and possibly St Petrock – and it is probable that the cult took root in the cathedral.[38] Certainly, by the late fifteenth century, the cathedral was observing another new feast of Christ, the Transfiguration, which was celebrated on 6 August, the day before the Feast of the Name.[39]

There are three or four other examples of cults directly related to God in the early Tudor cathedral. In about 1500 Precentor Sylke rebuilt the chapel of the Cross and decorated it with scenes of the Crucifixion. In the records for 1506 we read for the first time of an altar of the Holy Ghost, situated just off the cloister in the space between the south tower and the chapter house.[40] In 1514 Bishop Oldham (who helped to found Corpus Christi College, Oxford, also named after Christ) established an antiphon to be said in honour of the cross on the choir-screen.[41] At about the same time he built a new chapel for his burial-place in the south choir-aisle 'in the honour of my lord God and Saviour': St Saviour's, as it is now called.[42] All this is not to deny that the saints went on being honoured. Their feasts, altars and statues remained until the Reformation. We are simply drawing attention to a partial shift of interest: a little more directly towards God and a little away from the saints. The shift is significant in view of the approaching Reformation. The Protestant Church of England was to increase the emphasis on God in worship and to reduce the honour given to the saints. But the Reformation accelerated, rather than started, a change in fashion that had been developing for over a hundred years.

10

The Reformation

In the autumn of 1531 Exeter experienced a scandal such as nobody could remember. One October morning, papers containing controversial religious statements were found attached to the cathedral doors. The pope, they said, was the Antichrist, and no worship should be given to the saints. Antichrist was the evil ruler destined to appear towards the end of the world. The papers revealed the presence of a bold heretic in the city and the authorities set out to track him down – the bishop and clergy, we are told, as angry as wasps, the mayor and corporation demonstrating rather less zeal. Searches were made of some citizens' houses, and the unknown offender was solemnly excommunicated in the cathedral. About a week later an early worshipper en route to the Bratton mass at daybreak saw a boy attaching a document to the gate called Little Stile at the the north-east end of South Street. He seized the boy and took him to the mayor, where questioning soon showed that the boy was acting for his master, Thomas Benet, a local private schoolmaster. Benet was arrested at once and handed over to the clergy to be tried for heresy. He was examined at length by the bishop himself and other learned men and took no pains to hide his belief in Luther's teachings against the Catholic Church. This was heretical, and the heresy laws prescribed the death penalty for convicted heretics, though first offenders, if they retracted, could be let off. Benet refused all pleas and arguments to retract and in the end the law pursued its course. His case was reported to the Lord Chancellor in London, and eventually a writ commanding his execution arrived. He was burnt at the stake by the Sheriff of Devon outside the city at Livery Dole on 10 January 1532.[1]

Benet's case marks the start of a new chapter in cathedral history: the age of the Reformation. The views he held were soon to be officially adopted. Within three years the pope's authority in England was to be abolished and so, within twenty years, was the worship of saints. In 1531, however, such ideas were unfamiliar and rather unwelcome to most Exonians. There had been religious dissenters in England ever since Wycliffe in the 1370s, but scarcely any had appeared in Devon. Benet, significantly, was an immigrant scholar who had developed his opinions at Cambridge. He had a few sympathizers in Exeter, but only a few. Most local people, whether devoutly religious or not, were traditionalists. They were used to the established system of things and resented attempts to change it. John Hooker, who is

The Burning of Thomas Benet
The burning of Benet as it was later imagined in Protestant England. Not a true portrait, it simply aims to suggest the steadfastness of a godly man amid the flames.

our main informant about the Benet episode, admits that in 1531, 'few or none ... knew anything of God's matters' (i.e. Reformation matters). Indeed, at the burning, 'such was the devilish rage of the blind people, that well was he or she that could catch a stick or furze to cast into the fire'.[2] The clergy of the Close agreed with the laity. The bishop, John Veysey, was a conscientious man and himself a reformer, in the sense of keeping his diocese up to the mark. But he was not an adherent of the Reformation and went along with it only as far as he had to. The canons and lesser clergy numbered hardly anyone who favoured Protestantism, and more than one observer remarked on their conservatism. When the Reformation began, we are told, 'they were not inclined to the fashion of the world that goeth now', and wished instead that 'we should do as we have done in times past and live after the old fashion'.[3] This is not hard to understand. They had inherited a splendid building and an elaborate structure of services, both of which were in good working order. Their standard of living had never been better. The canons had their comfortable houses, and the vicars their college in Kalendarhay with their own chambers, dining-room and meals. The annuellars too were prospering. Four new chantries had been founded since 1500, and a house was set up in 1528 for all the chantry priests to live in.[4] Relations between the cathedral and its traditional enemies — the city and the friars — were stable and posed no serious problems. In many ways the 1510s and 1520s were an Indian summer for the Close before the storms to come. No wonder the clergy clung to their way of life and resisted attempts to change it.

There are some charming glimpses of the canons at this time in Hooker's history of Exeter, written later but based on his own reminiscences. The treasurer John Ryse was Hooker's godfather. A wealthy man, he used his money to provide facilities for the poorer cathedral clergy, and personally lived a simple and austere life far removed from our usual image of rich medieval prelates. Even in his eighties he wore shoes with one thin sole, refused to warm himself by the fire, 'and being advised by a friend that considering his age he should use warmer apparel, wear lined shoes and sit by the fire, he said, "What shall I then do when I am old?" ' The subdean Robert Weston was distinguished for his patronage of learning. He was 'a great benefactor of scholars', many of whom he helped through school or university with his money, including his nephews Nicholas, Richard and Robert. The first became a Bachelor of Divinity and succeeded his uncle as subdean, the second studied law and became a serjeant-at-law (leading barrister) and the third became Lord Chancellor of Ireland. Different again was William Parkhouse, Doctor of Medicine, who combined being canon with acting as a physician to local people. Being a cleric, he did not like to appear to charge for his services, so when he made out prescriptions he wrote underneath, for the chemist, 'Accipe pro te et me', meaning 'Charge him for thee and me'. In this way the patient unwittingly reimbursed the doctor when he paid the chemist. Parkhouse was a preacher too, though Hooker thought him more amusing than instructive. Robert Tregonwell was the heartiest of the canons. He saw no harm in keeping three or four good geldings in his stable or in hawking and hunting with water-spaniels, yet he was 'very well learned', gave theological lectures 'to his great commendation' and was one of the very few Exeter clergy with some sympathy for Luther. The evidence of Hooker, a Protestant writing after the Reformation who was not inclined to favour the old regime, is a testimony to the vitality of the cathedral community in the early 1530s. The best of the clergy were learned and sociable men, who kept up well the ancient duties of their calling: prayer, preaching and hospitality to others.[5]

Soon after 1530, however, the Indian summer began to fade. Disquieting news of strife and change was heard in the Close. There were reports of the king's divorce, attacks on the clergy in Parliament, a growing breach with the pope. In 1534 Henry VIII was proclaimed Head of the Church of England. Royal commissioners toured the country, including Exeter, and made every member of the clergy swear an oath repudiating the pope's authority and accepting that of the king. Propaganda was organized to win over the laity, and the government sent Hugh Latimer, the future Protestant martyr, round the West of England to preach in favour of Henry's Church reforms.[6] Latimer came to Exeter in June 1534 and caused a mild sensation. The local clergy treated him coldly, but nonetheless he preached three sermons that drew large crowds of lay people. The first was delivered in the churchyard of the Franciscan friary in Holloway Street; the friars would not let him in the church. Unfortunately, first there was a heavy shower and then the preacher's nose began to bleed, which some people took to be 'a sign of God's vengeance upon him for preaching of heresies'. The second sermon was preached in the Church of St Mary Major under protest from its clergy. So many people came that the building would not hold them all, and the church windows were broken open so that those outside could hear the preacher. The final sermon was delivered in the Close, not in the cathedral itself, which the canons managed to preserve inviolate, but from a pulpit in the charnel chapel near the west front. Once more a large crowd gathered to listen on the cathedral green, most of them quietly, but a local gentleman named Thomas Carew interrupted, calling Latimer a 'heretic knave', and bade him come down or else he would pull him by the ears. Latimer took this calmly and went on. His visit was a brief one, but it was symbolic. It signalled that reform of the Church (within limits) was now the official dogma. Two years earlier the traditionalists had been able to deal with Benet; now they were on the defensive and it was their turn to get into trouble if they stepped out of line.

The impact of the king's new role as head of the Church was gradually felt in other ways. Indulgences were never an issue in the English Reformation as they were in Germany, but they ended with the abolition of the pope's authority in 1534 and the cathedral lost the money they had produced. In the spring of 1535 every church had to submit a full statement of its revenue and expenditure to royal commissioners,[7] and this was soon followed by much heavier taxation of the clergy. Each cleric was made to pay the king a tenth of his income each year, and whenever he took up a new benefice, he had to pay the whole of its income for one year. Towards the end of 1535 John Tregonwell visited the cathedral on the king's behalf and ordered that the king's laws should take precedence over the cathedral statutes.[8] This was the first of a series of royal 'visitations' during the Tudor period. In 1536 Church authorities were forbidden to encourage pilgrimages, such as had been made to Bishop Lacy's tomb, and no one was to kneel or make offerings to images.[9]

Then, in 1537, the king stretched forth his hand against the chief member of the cathedral staff: the dean himself. For the last ten years this worthy had been Reginald Pole, who was the king's second cousin and the grandson of Edward IV's brother Clarence. Pole had long been in favour with Henry VIII and was elected dean in 1527 at the king's request.[10] He never came to Exeter and spent his time in Europe, studying at Paris and advising the pope on Church reforms. When Henry broke with Rome, he hoped to win Pole over to his side, but Pole remained in the papal camp and was made a cardinal. In the spring of 1537 Henry finally lost patience and deprived him of his benefices in England. This made the deanery of Exeter available for another royal nominee.

The local candidate was Thomas Brerewood, Archdeacon of Barnstaple. He was a strong candidate because he had been in the King's service and had the support of the Lord Chancellor, Thomas Audley. Audley lobbied Thomas Cromwell, the king's chief minister, and offered him £10 worth of wine to get the post for Brerewood, plus a present of £100 from Brerewood himself.[11] Cromwell was sympathetic, but either he changed his mind or Henry VIII expressed a different view, for in the end the deanery went to someone else altogether: Simon Heynes, sometime Vice-Chancellor of Cambridge University and President of Queens' College.[12] This caused the sort of reaction in Exeter which followed the appointment of Bishop Proudie in *Barchester Towers*. Heynes was an outsider without any local connections, a Cambridge man where the Exeter clergy were Oxonians, and a religious radical where they were largely conservatives. They knew or soon found out that Heynes had preached against the pope in Cambridge, entertained a Scottish reformer in his college and visited Germany to establish contact with the reformer Melanchthon. The news of the appointment was conveyed to Exeter by Richard Chamber, Heynes's 'Mr Slope', except that he was a layman. Not surprisingly, he got a cool reception. Bishop Veysey acted correctly, pointing out that Heynes would have to be appointed to a prebend first and elected to the deanery later, because only a prebendary could be elected dean. This involved a wait of three weeks to give the members of the chapter notice of the election. The other cathedral dignitaries, however, advised that Heynes should be given both prebend and deanery straight away, which Chamber thought was to make the appointment illegal and rescindable, but Veysey did not accept this advice. Chamber inspected the dean's house and found it in a poor state, because it had not been lived in for years. The garden was a wilderness and he had to pay 30s. to get it trimmed. He wrote to Heynes that the house would not be ready for three weeks or a month and that nobody in the area would offer to make mattresses! Sickness was raging in the city, too.[13] Heynes accordingly delayed his arrival a little. He was granted a prebend in his absence on 5 June, elected dean on 16 July, and was in residence in Exeter by 3 August.[14]

The dean and chapter did not like each other any better when they met. Heynes thought the local clergy 'very few of them well persuaded or well learned' and he did not care for many of the customs of the cathedral, particularly those which governed the rights of the dean.[15] The chapter could not fight him on religious matters, since he had the backing of the king and Cromwell, but they could do battle with him over cathedral customs, and this they very soon did. Disputes began within a month of Heynes's arrival and went on until the following January. The records show that Heynes claimed the traditional rights and powers of the deanery and made other, more dubious, demands. He wanted all the daily and quarterly payments canons received, but would not deposit the sum of £40 required from every canon taking up residence. He wished to be free to leave the cathedral for long periods, while retaining sole jurisdiction over cathedral property and a veto on the sealing of documents by the canons in chapter. He also had a personal objection to maintaining a light on the high altar in front of the consecrated host as previous deans had done. After many arguments, a compromise was finally reached on 12 January 1538. The dean was granted the payments he wanted, given a wide latitude of absence and not made to pay the £40 fee. In return, he had to moderate his claims to jurisdiction and to content himself with the powers of previous deans. Effectively, this meant that the dean could do much as he liked, provided it did not affect the rest of the chapter.[16]

Having secured the right to be away for long periods, Heynes proceeded to use it. He was more at home in London among other progressive clergymen than in Exeter, and in 1538 he was abroad for several months as an ambassador to the Emperor Charles V. He later returned to Devon, only to become involved in a second fracas, which may be called 'The Destruction of the Images'. In 1538 Thomas Cromwell ordered stronger measures to be taken to stop pilgrimages and offerings to images. Images which were 'abused' by people resorting to them were to be removed.[17] An attack was also made on the cult of St Thomas Becket, because he symbolized the triumph of the Church in an earlier struggle with the king. His festivals were abolished and all images and pictures of him were forbidden.[18] In 1539 and 1540, Heynes proceeded to put these orders into effect in Exeter Cathedral. First of all, he defaced the tomb of Bishop Lacy by tearing off the brass effigy of the bishop so as to render the tomb anonymous. Next (so the canons alleged) he destroyed several beautiful images of saints without consulting the chapter, although the images had not been treated superstitiously. In doing this he caused further damage to the cathedral walls and flooring. He lacerated books in the choir to the value of 20 marks (probably scoring out references to Becket and the pope) and, lastly, he took away the light on the high altar to which he had objected before although the king's laws tolerated it. In this way Heynes began the alteration of the cathedral interior, making it plainer and barer, and it is no wonder that the canons were angry.[19]

It would be unfair to Heynes, however, to present him merely as a sixteenth-century William Dowsing: a Puritan who went about the world destroying images. He was a learned and an able man, as his Cambridge posts and his royal embassy show, and he had a positive idea of what the cathedral should be like. In about 1540 (the exact date is not known) Heynes drew up a scheme for reforming the cathedral to submit to Henry VIII. Henry never acted on it, but it is interesting as the vision of a contemporary reformer and for the light it sheds on the way the cathedral functioned at the time. Like liberal churchmen today, Heynes thought that cathedrals spent too much time on prayer and not enough on social welfare and education. He aimed to correct this imbalance by reducing the number of clergy, thereby freeing money for other uses. The dean and twenty-four canons should, he felt, be replaced by a 'pastor' and twelve 'preachers', all of them divinity graduates. Their job would be to celebrate the daily services as before, preach on Sundays and go on preaching tours round other local churches. The thirty-eight vicars and annuellars should be reduced to only three priests, each charged with celebrating a dawn mass for early worshippers but no other masses. In place of the extra clergy there should be a theology lecturer, teaching three days a week, a free song-school, with a master teaching reading, singing and instrumental music, and a free grammar school, with two masters teaching Latin. Revenues were to be allocated to maintain a hundred children at the schools, twenty-four scholars at the universities and twenty-four almsmen. The cathedral would thus become like the colleges of Eton or Winchester, having a religious function but with the majority of its members engaged in study.

It is always interesting to see what limits reformers place on the changes they advocate. Heynes wished the new 'pastor' to keep all the legal powers of the dean over the cathedral clergy and the various local churches belonging to the cathedral. These were the very powers about which he was arguing with the canons! He had no concept of altering the privileged position of the cathedral and its churches within the diocese, and he wanted the revitalized canons or 'preachers' to go on entertaining visitors in their houses. Even Heynes could not imagine (or dared not suggest) a cathedral without wealthy clergy offering hospitality to other people.[20]

For three years there was little that Heynes's opponents could do to thwart his projects. He remained in favour with the king and with Cromwell, and in 1539 was appointed a member of the short-lived Council of the West, set up to rule the South West of England. But in the summer of 1540 things began to change. In the previous year Henry VIII had put a brake on the Reformation with the 'Act of Six Articles', which confirmed several Catholic beliefs. Then, in June 1540, came the fall of Cromwell, and the strengthening of the conservative group in the king's Privy Council. This altered the political climate in England, leaving Heynes and his henchmen weak and unprotected. The canons of Exeter could at last take the initiative. Their first action came on 24 July, when they revoked the powers they had given Heynes to represent the cathedral at Parliament.[21] At about the same time they seem to have stopped his allowances. When Heynes came back to Exeter in September he had to ask for his allowances to be restored, but the canons replied that he owed the exchequer £40 (the unpaid entry fee, perhaps) and would have to pay this first. When Heynes agreed, they made five further charges against him, based on his damage to the images. Heynes denied the charges probably feeling that he could justify his actions, and it was decided to put the matter to arbitration.[22] What happened next is not clear, but Heynes was in a beleaguered state. He went away again at Christmas 1541 and was still absent in March 1542, when the chapter resolved not to grant him any allowances for the period concerned and promised to stand together if he took the matter to law.[23] The nadir of Heynes's fortunes came a year later, when he was ordered to present himself before the Privy Council on 16 March. By this time the government was out to deal with him, and when he arrived he was committed to the Fleet prison for holding 'evil opinions' in favour of

Lutheranism and heresy. How they must have gloated over the news in Exeter: the dean in prison for heresy! During the following months evidence was collected against Heynes, and the Privy Council asked the bishop and chapter for information. In the end, either he made a grovelling submission or the charges could not be made to stick, for on 5 July he was pardoned. He was brought back before the Council, reprimanded for 'sowing erroneous opinions', but told of the king's mercy. He was then bound over for the huge sum of 5000 marks and released.[24]

For the last three years of Henry's reign Heynes lived partly in Exeter and partly elsewhere. He was careful to avoid offending the canons, and the two parties managed to rub along together a little better. Indeed, at the end of 1544, the canons even reappointed Heynes to be one of their proctors at convocation in London. Perhaps they remembered, as people in Tudor times often did, that the present monarch could not live for ever and that the next one might have different views of religion. This is exactly what happened after Henry's death in 1547. The government of the young Edward VI was dominated by Reformers and soon began to carry the Reformation further in a Protestant direction. Heynes, of course, came back into favour at once. He was made a Justice of the Peace and one of four royal commissioners charged with reforming the Church in the West of England, and when he came with his colleagues to Exeter Cathedral on 23 October 1547, he at last held full powers to deal with the canons. In the event, he treated them less harshly than one might have expected. Of course, he was only the government's servant, enforcing its pre-arranged policy, so he could not do absolutely what he liked. Perhaps he had been chastened by his battles and mellowed by the greater harmony of recent years. More certainly, he had a skeleton in his cupboard that could still cause him embarrassment. He had contracted a secret marriage, or at any rate a liaison, with a certain Joan Wallron, who bore him a son at about this time. Marriage for clergymen did not become legal until 1549 and was still much frowned upon. This fact may well have caused Heynes to behave more moderately at his visitation than his opponents must have feared.

The royal visitors of 1547 shared Heynes's earlier view that cathedrals needed less prayer and more education, but they did not make as many changes as he had recommended.[25] The resident canons were largely left alone, except that for the first time they were ordered to preach sermons every Sunday, turn and turn about. In compensation for this duty, their attendance at daily worship was cut down to one service only: matins, high mass, or evensong. The number of vicars choral was maintained at twenty, but in future only eight of these were to be priests, the other twelve being recruited from laymen. Instead of continuing as regular members of the choir, the twelve secondaries were to become scholars at the city grammar school, attending the choir on Sundays and festival days. The choristers were to receive three meals a day in the vicars' college in Kalendarhay rather than going individually to the canons' houses. This was a long-overdue reform that had nothing to do with Protestantism. An attempt was made to involve the cathedral in public education. The city grammar school in the High Street, which had previously had little connection with the cathedral, was now put under the control of the chapter. This brought with it the responsibility for appointing and paying the masters, and was an unpopular burden because of the expense involved. After a few years the arrangement was quietly dropped. Exeter never acquired a permanent cathedral grammar school and the present cathedral prep school is a modern development.[26] The visitors did not concern themselves with the annuellars, but six months later, at Easter 1548, all chantries throughout England were abolished and their clergy pensioned off. The eighteen surviving annuellars disappeared from the choir and their daily masses ceased to be said at the cathedral altars.[27]

By 1548, therefore, the number of resident cathedral clergy had fallen, and those who were required to attend the choir on weekdays were even fewer. In 1549 the services themselves were altered, the medieval Latin service-books were abolished and the first English prayer book – the Book of Common Prayer – was introduced.[28] The prayer-book changed both the language of worship (from Latin to English) and the form of worship. The eight medieval services which had been said in the choir were reduced to two – matins and evensong – and the services in honour of Our Lady and the dead were dropped. All religious processions, inside the cathedral on Sundays and outside in the spring, were also discontinued, as were all the picturesque religious ceremonies: ashes on Ash Wednesday, palms on Palm Sunday, foot-washing on Maundy Thursday, creeping to the cross on Good Friday and so on.[29] The boy-bishop service on 28 December had already been suppressed in 1543.[30] The mass remained, under the new name of 'communion service', but it was said less frequently than before. Private communion services were prohibited and only corporate ones, involving all the clergy, were allowed. We do not know what the daily pattern of cathedral services was immediately after 1549, but ten years later it was organized as follows. At 6 a.m. there was a series of prayers replacing the Bratton mass at daybreak: the confession, the Litany and a lesson from the New Testament. At 7.45 the clergy gathered in the choir, where they said matins. At 9 a.m. one of the clergy read a divinity lecture, or a commentary on the gospels, and at 10 a.m. the communion service was held, so that the clergy still spent most of morning in church.[31] After dinner, in place of vespers and compline there was evensong in the choir. Therefore, despite the changes brought by the Reformation, the ancient pattern of the day survived in a recognizable form.

The splendour of the worship, however, was greatly diminished after 1549. The new setting was a plain, indeed a ravaged, one. The great stone reredos behind the high altar was robbed of the images of Christ and the saints that had embellished it, and so were the sedilia and the bishop's throne beside it. The high altar with its silver fittings was replaced by a wooden table, and the other altars were removed altogether, along with all the portable wooden images. The Lady chapel and the other chapels were left empty and unused, their dedications forgotten, and some of them were turned into vestries or court-rooms; the charnel chapel in the Close was pulled down. Needless damage was done, in the Heynes tradition. Bishop Berkeley's tomb was stripped of its brass and Bishop Grandisson's was completely destroyed. Most of the silver and gold was confiscated and the relics were thrown away. None of the embroidered altar-frontals was retained, or the rich vestments for mass and processions, and clerical dress was limited to a surplice over a black cassock. A medieval vestment bearing the arms of Grandisson and the Keys

The Empty Cathedral
The area in front of the choir-screen in the nineteenth century, much as it was left after the Reformation. The statues and altars which stood on and around the screen have all been removed.

of St Peter is still kept in the Portuguese islands of the Azores. It presumably found its way there from Exeter Cathedral after 1549, but it is a rare survivor of the devastation.)[32] Sensitive people, then and for decades afterwards, regretted the damage done at the Reformation; two generations later John Donne likened the Church of England to a woman 'robbed and torn'.[33]

The 1540s are a suitable point at which end this book. True, there was a return to Catholic worship under Mary in 1553, but it was short-lived, and when Elizabeth succeeded in 1558 the changes of the 1540s were confirmed in most respects. Still, perhaps the things that did not change are as remarkable as the changes themselves. The cathedral survived as an institution. It preserved its buildings largely intact, and it held on to its canons and some of its lesser clergy, its estates, its walled and gated Close and its privileged status in the City and the diocese. In addition, like a cut-back plant, it retained sufficient energy to make up for its losses with new growth. The building, in particular, continued to cast such a spell that later generations were moved to repair the damage done at the Reformation, and much has been restored or replaced: altars, chapels, paintings, fittings, plate and vestments. Indeed, the Reformation can be said to have enhanced the English cathedrals in the long run. Previously they had not been the only great churches of the nation. Many abbeys, such as Fountains, Glastonbury and Walsingham, equalled or surpassed them as buildings and pilgrimage centres. Even in Exeter the cathedral had to compete with six smaller priories and friaries for the devotion and money of local people. When Henry VIII dissolved the monasteries he removed this competition and left the field to the cathedrals. Their present popularity could not have been as great if the abbeys had remained, for its rests on their uniqueness as well as their beauty.

And Heynes? He died in his late fifties, between July and November 1552, probably at Windsor (where he was a canon) or at Westminster (where he owned a house). After 1547 he had largely withdrawn from Exeter,[34] and only one of the cathedral staff was mentioned in his will: the chapter clerk, John Ryder, who would have transacted business for him.[35] Heynes left his property to his wife – their marriage had for some time been openly acknowledged – and to their two young sons, Joseph and Simon; his will suggests a devoted husband and father. He did not say where he wished to be buried and his final resting-place is not recorded, but one thing is certain: it was not in the cathedral. In this respect, at least, he showed some tact.

Notes

Virtually all the books referred to will be found in the University of Exeter library catalogue, and the odd exceptions in the British Library Catalogue (housed in the University library).

Abbreviations

Accounts of the Fabric	*The Accounts of the Fabric of Exeter Cathedral, 1279–1353*, ed. Audrey M. Erskine, 2 parts, Devon and Cornwall Record Society, new series, xxiv, xxvi (1981–3).
D&C	Exeter Cathedral Archives, Dean and Chapter records.
DRO	Devon Record Office, Exeter.
f., ff.	folio(s).
Oliver	G. Oliver, *Lives of the Bishops of Exeter and a History of the Cathedral*, Exeter, 1861.
Ordinale	*Ordinale Exon*, ed. J.N. Dalton and G.H. Doble, 4 vols, Henry Bradshaw Society, xxxvii–viii, lxiii, lxxix (1909–40).
p., pp.	page(s).
Reg.	The published registers of the medieval bishops: Bronescombe, Stapeldon, Grandisson, Brantyngham and Stafford, ed. F.C. Hingeston-Randolph, 8 vols, London and Exeter, 1886–1906; Lacy's *Registrum Commune*, ed. G.R. Dunstan, 5 vols, Devon and Cornwall Record Society, new series, vii, x, xiii, xvi, xviii (1963–72).
s.a.	*sub anno*, i.e. 'under the year' in D&C accounts without page references.
v	verso.

Chapter 1: The Close

1. On the Close in general, *see* Ethel Lega-Weekes, *Some Studies in the Topography of the Cathedral Close, Exeter*, Exeter, 1915.
2. John Hooker, *The Description of the City of Excester*, ed. W.J. Harte and others, 3 parts, Devon and Cornwall Record Society, 1919–47, ii, 215–16, describes the situation in the sixteenth century, which may be traced back to the mid-twelfth century in D&C 1374 and 2074.
3. For references to bell-ringing fees, *see* D&C 3773 ff.54^V, 70–^{V}.
4. Hooker, *Description*, ii, 213, 215–16.
5. *Oliver*, pp. 167–8.
6. D&C 3530, between ff. 59–60.
7. Hooker, *Description*, ii, 212.
8. D&C 2920.
9. Hooker, *Description*, ii, 217–22.
10. *See* Chapter 5, note 49.
11. On what follows, *see* Frances Rose-Troup, *The Lost Chapels of Exeter*, Exeter, 1923, *passim*.

12. Two lists of Exeter chapels, c. 1194–1215, which proceed in strict topographical order, place St Mary Minor next to St Mary Major (*The Lost Chapels of Exeter*, pp. 17–19). It lay, perhaps, in the Close near Little Stile, in the territory which later belonged to the parish of St Mary Major.
13. *John Lydford's Book*, ed. Dorothy M. Owen, London, Historical MSS Commission and Devon and Cornwall Record Society, new series, xx (1974), p. 105. Cf. D&C 3550 f. 130^V.
14. *Letters & Papers of John Shillingford*, ed. S.A. Moore, London, Camden Society, new series, ii (1871), p. 89; Hooker, *Description*, ii. 221.
15. Frances Rose-Troup, *Exeter Vignettes*, Manchester, 1942, p. 46.
16. C.G. Henderson and P.T. Bidwell, 'The Saxon Minster at Exeter', *The Early Church in Western Britain and Ireland*, ed. Susan M. Pearce, Oxford, 1982, pp. 168–9.
17. D&C 3550 f. 72^V; *Letters of Shillingford*, ed. Moore, p. 101.
18. D&C 3550 f. 21.
19. On bonfires, *see* Chapter 8, note 29.
20. Lega-Weekes, *Cathedral Close*, pp.22–3, 27–8.
21. *Reg. Brantyngham*, i, 333–4; ii, 616–17, 688.
22. D&C 2920.
23. E.g. *Reg. Grandisson*, ii, 983–4, 1163–5; *Reg. Brantyngham*, i, 157, 159, 169; ii, 583.
24. On the bishop's fee, *see* Muriel L. Curtis, *Some Disputes between the City and the Cathedral Authorities of Exeter*, Manchester, 1932, pp. 9–19.
25. On what follows, *see* Rose-Troup, *Exeter Vignettes*, pp. 38–57.
26. *Calendar of Patent Rolls, 1281–92*, p. 215.
27. Hooker, *Description*, ii, 156–61.
28. *Accounts of the Fabric*, ii, 240; N. Orme, *The Minor Clergy of Exeter Cathedral*, Exeter, 1980, p. 10.
29. *Cathedral of Close Rolls, 1339–41*, p. 350.
30. *Letters of Shillingford*, ed. Moore. On what follows, *see* ibid. pp. 75–114, and Curtis, *Disputes, passim*.
31. Ibid., pp. 71–6.
32. John Vowell alias Hooker, *A Catalog of the Bishops of Excester*, London, 1584.
33. D&C 2864.
34. Hooker, *Catalog*, f. Aij.

Chapter 2: The Cathedral

1. *Reg. Brantyngham*, ii, 713.
2. William Worcestre, *Itineraries*, ed. J.H. Harvey, Oxford, 1969. pp. 116–17.
3. Geoffrey of Monmouth, *Historia Regum Britanniae*, ed. A. Griscom, London and New York, 1929, p. 325; *The History of the Kings of Britain*, trans. L. Thorpe, Harmondsworth, Penguin, 1966, p. 122.
4. *Letters of Shillingford*, ed. Moore, pp. 75–6.
5. For the 'table', *see* ibid., p. 105; Worcestre, *Itineraries*, pp. 116–17; and Hooker, *Catalog of Bishops*, f. Aij. Extracts from the table quoted in these sources show that it was identical with the 'Brief Exeter Chronicle' in D&C 3625 ff. 54^V–59, partially printed in *Ordinale*, i, pp. xix–xxiii.
6. *Vitae Sancti Bonifatii*, ed. W. Levison, Monumenta Germaniae Historica, Scriptores Rerum Germanicorum, Hannover and Leipzig, 1905, p. 7; C.H. Talbot, *The Anglo-Saxon Missionaries in Germany*, London, 1954, p. 28.

7. *Ordinale*, iii, 247–8.
8. D&C 3521, p. 261; N. Orme in *The Greatest Englishman*, ed. T. A. Reuter, Exeter, 1980, pp. 107–8.
9. On the following topics, *see* Henderson and Bidwell in *The Early Church in Britain and Ireland*, ed. Pearce, pp. 145–175.
10. P. Chaplais, 'The Authenticity of the Royal Anglo-Saxon Diplomas of Exeter', *Bulletin of the Institute of Historical Research*, xxxix (1966), pp. 1–9.
11. D&C 3673 (obit); *see* p. 83 (relics); H.E. Bishop and Edith K. Prideaux, *The Building of the Cathedral Church of St Peter in Exeter*, Exeter, 1922, pp. 161–2. (glass). Athelstan is called the 'first founder' by William Worcestre, *Itineraries*, pp. 116–17.
12. Henderson and Bidwell, op cit., p. 159.
13. On Leofric, *see* F. Barlow et al., *Leofric of Exeter*, Exeter,1972, pp. 1–16.
14. *The Exeter Book of Old English Poetry*, ed. R.W. Chambers et al., London, 1933, pp. 18–30.
15. Oxford, Bodleian Library, MS Digby 81 ff. 66, 88; Rose-Troup, *Exeter Vignettes*, p. 24.
16. For a discussion of the plan, *see* the note on p. 116.
17. On this topic, *see* p. 39.
18. D&C 600; Oliver, pp. 417–18 (misdated 1237).
19. *See* note on p. 116.
20. I.e. St John the Evangelist, St Gabriel, St Andrew, St Katherine, St Mary Magdalene and St James (*see* pp. 84–5).
21. *Accounts of the Fabric*, i, 6–7; ii, p. xxvii.
22. Now published to 1353 in *Accounts of the Fabric*.
23. *Ordinale*, i, p. xxii.
24. *Accounts of the Fabric*, i, 1–3; ii, pp. ix, xxvi.
25. *Reg. Grandisson*, i, 434.
26. The remainder of this chapter is based on Mrs Erskine's excellent synthesis in *Accounts of the Fabric*, ii, pp. ix–xxxvi.
27. Ibid., ii, 330 (index to references). On 'Old Peter', *see also* pp. 26–7.
28. *See* p. 99.

Chapter 3: The Inside

1. *Accounts of the Fabric*, ii, pp. xxxii, 238–9, 245–6, 253.
2. *Letters of Shillingford*, ed. Moore, pp. 86, 101.
3. N. Orme, 'The Medieval Chantries of Exeter Cathedral, II and III', *Devon and Cornwall Notes and Queries*, xxxv (1982), pp. 14–15.
4. D&C 3773 f. 71; 3678 f. 5^V.
5. Oliver, pp. 466, 475.
6. *See* below, pp. 75–8.
7. *Reg. Lacy*, iv. 24.
8. D&C 3551 ff. 29–^{V}, 79.
9. *Ordinale*, i, 293–4, 323.
10. Orme in *Devon and Cornwall Notes and Queries*, xxxv (1982), pp. 17–18.
11. D&C 4037 (*The Ichnography of the Cathedral Church of St Peter at Exeter*, published by J. Jones, 1757).
12. So Oliver suggested (p. 217), from the will of Richard Martyn (DRO, Chanter XII (i) f. 137^V).
13. N. Orme, 'The Medieval Chantries of Exeter Cathedral, I', *Devon and Cornwall Notes and Queries*, xxxiv (1981), pp. 322–3; xxxv (1982), pp. 13–15.

14. D&C 2920; 3678 ff. 1^V-2^V.
15. *Ordinale*, i, 294, 311, 319; D&C 3773 ff. 13-50; 3779 ff. 62^V-135^V *passim*.
16. DRO, Exeter Receivers' Accounts, 1-2 Henry VIII.
17. *Ordinale*, ii, 539.
18. On what follows, *see* D&C 2920; 3678.
19. D&C 2657; 3678 f. 3.
20. D&C 2413.
21. Orme in *Devon and Cornwall Notes and Queries*, xxxiv (1981), pp. 322-4; xxxv (1982), pp. 14-16, 18-19, 67.
22. Ibid., xxxiv (1981), p. 323.
23. *Ordinale*, i, 74, 76.
24. D&C 2920; 3678 ff. 1^V, 11^V.
25. Ibid., f. 6.
26. *Accounts of the Fabric*; 1, 52, 62; ii, 259, 267.
27. On the cult, *see* N. Orme, 'Two Saint-Bishops of Exeter: James Berkeley and Edmund Lacy', *Analecta Bollandiana*, civ (1986), forthcoming.
28. *Reg. Lacy*, i, 169; there is no reference in 1506 in Oliver, pp. 320-76.
29. *Reg. Lacy*, iv, 23.
30. On the exchequer, *see* Audrey M. Erskine, 'The Medieval Financial Records of the Cathedral Church of Exeter', *Journal of the Society of Archivists*, ii part vi (1962), pp. 254-66.
31. *Reg. Lacy*, iv, 60.
32. D&C 3764 f. 22; 3766 *s.a.* 1357; 2920; 3678 f. 11^V; DRO, Exeter City Act Book I f. 93 (13 Henry VIII).
33. *See* note 27.
34. D&C 2190.
35. Oliver, pp. 352-3.
36. Orme in *Devon and Cornwall Notes and Queries*, xxxiv (1981), pp. 321 (*bis*), 322; xxxv (1982), p. 68; Public Record Office, Prob. 11/19 f. 148 (the will of Hugh Oldham).
37. On the screen, high altar and east end, *see* Percy Morris, 'Exeter Cathedral: A Conjectural Reconstruction of the Fourteenth-Century Altar Screen', *The Antiquaries Journal*, xxiii (1943), pp. 122-47; xxiv (1944), pp. 10-21.
38. A box of St Peter 'at the horn of the high altar' is mentioned in 1524 (D&C 3686 f. 89^V), and one at the feet of St Paul for the Berkeley offerings in 1334 (D&C 3764 f. 95).
39. Oliver, pp. 331, 334, 359-60.

Chapter 4: The Clergy

1. On cathedrals in general, *see* Kathleen Edwards, *The English Secular Cathedrals in the Middle Ages*, 2nd edn, Manchester, 1967, especially pp. 1-32.
2. On the movements of medieval bishops of Exeter, *see Reg. Bronescombe*, pp. 294-302, 383-6; *Reg. Stapeldon*, pp. 547-60; *Reg. Grandisson*, iii, 1524-32; *Reg. Brantyngham*, ii, 890-6; and *Reg. Stafford*, pp. 476-9.
3. For references to the bishop in cathedral worship, *see Ordinale*, iv, 212 (index).
4. For the statutes, *see* D&C 3625 ff. $1-54^V$; Oliver, pp. 465-9, 471-6.
5. *See* pp. 66-70.
6. *See* e.g. *Reg. Grandisson*, ii, 857-63.
7. Ibid., iii, 1512-13.

8.   William Warelwast (d. 1137) was buried in Plympton Priory, which he founded;
     John Bothe (d. 1478 at East Horsley, Surrey) in the parish church there; John
     Arundel (d. 1504 at his London house) in St Clement Dane's church near by in
     The Strand; and John Veysey (d. 1554 at Sutton Coldfield) in its parish
     church. It is not certain where Robert II (d. 1160), Bartholomew (d. 1184) and
     Richard Blund (d. 1257) are buried, but the cathedral is most likely.

9.   *The Old English Version of the Enlarged Rule of Chrodegang*, ed. A.S. Napier,
     London, Early English Text Society, original series, cl (1916) pp. 12-16, 19-21.

10. On what follows, *see* Erskine in *Journal of the Society of Archivists*, ii (1962),
     especially pp. 254-60.

11. D&C 3625 ff. 6-7^V, 8-11.

12. *The Rule of St Chrodegang*, pp. 21-30.

13. On what follows, *see* Audrey M. Erskine, 'Bishop Briwere and the
     Reorganization of the Chapter of Exeter Cathedral', *Devonshire Association
     Transactions*, cviii (1976), pp. 159-71.

14. D&C 975.

15. On the dean's and other dignitaries' duties, *see also Ordinale*, i, 3-5.

16. N. Orme, *Education in the West of England, 1066-1548*, Exeter, 1976, pp. 52-3.

17. Oliver, pp. 468, 475-6.

18. On the canons' houses, *see* D&C 3673 f. 17-^{V}, printed in *Reg. Stapeldon*, pp.
     153-4, and D. Portman, *Exeter Houses, 1400-1600*, Exeter, 1966, pp. 7-8,
     66-73, fix. ix.

19. On the fruit-trees, *see* D&C 3550 ff. 20^V, 91.

20. On this and the following data, *see* the canons' wills in *Reg. Stafford*, pp.
     379-423.

21. *Reg. Grandisson*, i, 435.

22. On the clerical day, *see* Chapter 7.

23. D&C 3625, f. 9-^{V}.

24. Ibid.; *Ordinale*, i, 6.

25. N. Orme, 'Education and Learning at a Medieval English Cathedral: Exeter,
     1380-1548', *Journal of Ecclesiastical History*, xxxii (1981), p. 282.

26. On learning at the cathedral, *see* ibid., pp. 265-83 *passim*.

27. On these writers, *see* A.B. Emden, *A Biographical Register of the University
     of Oxford to A.D. 1500*, 3 vols, Oxford, 1957-9, i, 240-41, 298-9; ii, 1329-30.

28. *Reg. Grandisson*, i, 435; ii, 858, 985-6; *Reg Brantyngham*, i, 470; ii, 664;
     Oliver, pp. 467-8, 472.

29. Ibid., pp. 467-8.

30. Ibid., p. 472.

31. D&C 3625 f. 4-^{V}.

32. The following pages on the minor clergy are based on Orme, *Minor Clergy*, and
     'The Medieval Clergy of Exeter Cathedral', *Devonshire Association
     Transactions*, cxiii (1981), pp. 79-102; cxv (1983), pp. 79-100.

33. On the Exeter guild of Kalendars and the meaning of Kalendarhay, *see* N.
     Orme, 'The Kalendar Brethren of the City of Exeter', *Devonshire Association
     Transactions*, cix (1977), pp. 153-69.

34. *See* note 25, pp. 282-3.

35. *Reg. Brantyngham*, i, 470; Oliver, p. 468.

36. *Letters & Papers, Foreign & Domestic, Henry VIII*, v, 733-4; *Reg. Stafford*,
     pp. 379, 382, 389, 402, 411; *Reg. Lacy*, iv, 39, 63.

37. *See* p. 8; Curtis, *Disputes*, pp. 23-5.

38. *See* pp. 80-81.

39. D&C 3673; 3764-3772.

40. *See* N. Orme, 'The Cathedral Cat', *Friends of Exeter Cathedral, Fifty-First
     Annual Report* (1981), pp. 11-13.

Chapter 5: The King

1. Except for William III.
2. For details of episcopal appointments, *see* J. Le Neve, *Fasti Ecclesiae Anglicanae, 1300*–1541, vol. ix: *Exeter Diocese*, ed. Joyce M. Horn, London, 1964, pp. 1–3.
3. Ibid., *passim*.
4. Ibid., p. 24; *Reg. Stapeldon*, pp. 13–14, 273.
5. Le Neve, *Fasti, passim*. For their careers, *see* Emden, *Register of Oxford to 1500*.
6. D&C 3498/22.
7. Ibid., /56, 58.
8. Ibid., /65.
9. Le Neve, *Fasti*, pp. 5, 21.
10. *The Sarum Missal*, ed. J. Wickham Legge, Oxford, 1916, p. 221.
11. *Reg. Bronescombe*, p. 326.
12. D&C 2162.
13. D&C 1848; Oliver, pp. 486, 460.
14. D&C 3673 f. 62^V; Oliver, p. 487; D&C 3550 f. 14.
15. D&C 3770 sub Easter term, 1414 (fragmentary), 1415. One should also mention the celebration of royal births (Edward III in 1312, D&C 3673 f. 116^V) and funerals (*Ordinale*, ii, 538), including Emperor Sigismund, 1438 (*Proceedings and Ordinances of the Privy Council of England*, ed. N.H. Nicolas, vol. v, London, 1835, p. 88), Prince Arthur, 1502 (D&C 3779 f. 95), and Jane Seymour, 1537 (ibid., f. 148^V).
16. M.T. Clanchy, *From Memory to Written Record*, London, 1979, p. 213.
17. *Reg. Grandisson*, ii, 1173–4; iii, 1190–91, 1200–1201; *Reg. Brantyngham*, i, 187, 190–91, 199, 299, 343, 432; ii, 639, 656; *Reg. Stafford*, pp. 128–9; *Reg. Lacy*, i, 38–42, 85, 109–11, 116, 149–51; ii, 15–17, 156, 283–5.
18. D&C 2688.
19. D&C 2864.
20. What follows supplements the original work on this subject: J. Gidley, *Notices of Exeter comprising a History of Royal Visits*, Exeter, 1863.
21. D.C. Douglas, *William the Conqueror*, London, 1964, p. 213.
22. D&C 3672 p. 34; *Regesta Regum Anglo-Normanorum, 1066–1154*, vol. iii, ed. H.A. Cronne and R.H.C. Davis, Oxford, 1968, pp. 107–8.
23. H. Gough, *Itinerary of King Edward the First*, 2 Vols, Paisley, 1900, i, 174; ii, 17; Rose-Troup, *Exeter Vignettes*, pp. 49–50; M.A.E. Green, *Lives of the Princesses of England*, 6 vols, London, 1849–55, ii, 292–5.
24. Gough, *Itinerary*, ii, 152–3.
25. Green, *Lives of the Princesses*, iii, 250.
26. D&C 3766 *s.a.* 1349.
27. *Register of Edward the Black Prince*, 4 vols, London, 1930–33, ii, 66–70; iii, 175–7; iv, 143–68.
28. *Chronica Johannis de Reading et Anonymi Cantuariensis*, ed. J. Tait, Manchester, 1914, pp. 126, 204, 267–8 (where other chronicle sources are given). Jean Froissart, *Chroniques*, ed. Kervyn de Lettenhove, 25 vols, Brussels, 1867–77, vi, 13–17, who alleges that the prince landed at Dover or Sandwich, is therefore incorrect.
29. *Register of Edward*, ii, 192–203; iii, 452–8; iv, 465–501.
30. Froissart, *Chroniques*, viii, 60–63. In one version Froissart more or less correctly speaks of the prince sailing to Cornwall (p. 61), but in another version he is again incorrect in suggesting Southampton (p. 63).
31. *The Anonimalle Chronicle, 1333 to 1381*, ed. V.H. Galbraith, 2nd edn, Manchester, 1970, p. 67.

32. D&C 3767 *s.a.* 1371; DRO, Exeter, Book 51 f. 284[V].
33. *John of Gaunt's Register, 1372–1376*, ed. S. Armitage-Smith, 2 vols, London, Royal Historical Society, Camden third series, xx–xxi (1911), i, 4, 56, 94, 160; ii, 10–12, 297.
34. D&C 3767 *s.a.* 1371.
35. Cecily Radford, 'An Unrecorded Royal Visit to Exeter', *Devonshire Association Transactions*, lxiii (1931), pp. 255–63.
36. B.P. Wolffe, *Henry VI*, London, 1981, pp. 259–60, 369–70.
37. DRO, Exeter, Book 51 ff. 309[V]–10[V].
38. C.D. Ross, *Edward IV*, London, 1974. pp. 139–45.
39. DRO, Exeter, Book 51 f. 316–[V]. On the Palm Sunday processions, *see* p. 77.
40. D&C 3778 sub 12 Dec 1470.
41. Ross, *Edward IV*, p. 169.
42. D&C 3778 sub 1471; DRO, Exeter, Book 51 f. 317[V].
43. C.D. Ross, *Richard III*, London, 1981, pp. 109–17; DRO, Exeter, Book 51 ff. 322[V]–3.
44. *See* p. 61.
45. J. Gairdner, *History of Richard III*, 2nd edn., Cambridge, 1898, pp. 329–30.
46. Public Record Office, E 101/414/16 ff. 1[V]–4[V]; S. Bentley, *Excerpta Historica*, London, 1831, p. 114.
47. DRO, Exeter, Book 51, f. 329[V].
48. *Calendar of State Papers Spanish*, i, 262.
49. DRO, Exeter, Book 51, f. 330[V].
50. D&C 3680 sub Dec 1502.

Chapter 6: The People

1. Hooker, *Catalog*, f. Ei.
2. *Reg. Grandisson*, ii, 785.
3. *See* p. 1.
4. D&C 3625 f. 117; *Ordinale*, ii, 544.
5. *Reg. Grandisson*, ii, 785–6.
6. For the amounts, *see* below, p. 60.
7. D&C 2190; *Calendar of Papal Letters*, Vol iii: *1342*–1362, p. 139; *Reg. Lacy*, i, 144.
8. Oliver, p. 249.
9. John Smyth, *The Berkeley Manuscripts. The Lives of the Berkeleys*, ed. Sir J. Maclean, 2 vols, Gloucester, 1883–5, i, 218.
10. *See* pp. 25, 28.
11. D&C 3765 *s.a.* 1338, 1341.
12. *Reg. Grandisson*, ii, 941–2.
13. Quarterly figures of offerings are given in D&C 3673; 3764–3772.
14. *See* pp. 26, 29.
15. *Reg. Brantyngham*, ii, 665; *see also* p. 70.
16. *Ordinale*, i, 293–4.
17. D&C 2864.
18. D&C 3673 f. 88[V]; *Ordinale*, i, 74, 76, 112, 311.
19. *See* pp. 75–6.
20. *Ordinale*, i, 138.
21. *Accounts of the Fabric*, i, 1, 52, 125, 146; ii, 234, 243; D&C 3764 *s.a.* 1325; 3765 *s.a.* 1344, 1345; 3773 f. 54[V].
22. D&C 3673; 3764–3772.

23. On what follows, *see* Orme in *Analecta Bollandiana*, civ (1986), forthcoming.
24. Ursula M. Radford, 'The Wax Images found in Exeter Cathedral', *The Antiquaries Journal*, xxix (1949), pp. 164–8.
25. *Reg. Brantyngham*, i, 490–91.
26. (Thomas Walsingham), *Chronicon Angliae*, ed. E.M. Thompson, London, Rolls Series, 1874, p. 377.
27. D&C 3625 f. 19^V.
28. Oliver, p. 309.
29. *A Relation ... of the Island of England*, ed. Charlotte A. Sneyd, London, Camden Society, xxxvii (1847), p. 23.
30. D&C 2413.
31. What follows is based on a study of the obit accounts, D&C 3673; 3764–3772, and the fabric accounts, D&C 2602–2704/7. There are also a few mentions of offerings in D&C 3773 ff. 54^V, 70^V, 71, and 3774/undated fragments f. 3^V.
32. D&C 3501 f.7–^{V}; *The Exeter Book*, ed. Chambers, pp. 53–4.
33. E.g. *Devon Feet of Fines*, ed. O.J. Reichel, 2 vols, Exeter, Devon and Cornwall Record Society 1912–39, i, 129–30, 279, 285; ii, 45, D&C 2162; *Accounts of the Fabric*, ii, 235, 244.
34. Oliver, p. 249.
35. For examples of lay business, *see* D&C 3550 f. 70^V; Curtis, *Disputes*, pp. 84–5; Lambeth Palace Library, Reg. John Morton, i, f. 121.
36. William Caxton, *The Book of the Knight of the Tower*, ed. M.Y. Offord, London, Early English Text Society, supplementary series, ii (1971), pp. 59–60, 165–6.
37. *Rotuli Parliamentorum*, ed. J. Strachey, 6 vols, London, 1767–77, vi, 454–5.
38. *Reg. Brantyngham*, i, 490–91; D&C 3550 f. 20^V.
39. D&C 3625 ff. 121^V–2; *Ordinale*, ii, 548.
40. *Reg. Grandisson*, ii, 891–4.
41. Ibid., pp. 1163–5.
42. *Letters of Shillingford*, ed. Moore, pp. 78, 83, 97.
43. *Reg. Lacy*, i, 317–19.
44. On these episodes, *see* R.L. Storey, *The End of the House of Lancaster*, London, 1966, pp. 165–75.
45. On what follows, *see Calendar of Inquisitions Post Mortem*, xv, 296–7; *Calendar of Patent Rolls, 1381–5*, 242; *Reg. Brantyngham*, i, 490–91.

Chapter 7: The Day

1. Beatrix F. Cresswell, *The Edwardian Inventories for Exeter*, London, Alcuin Club Collections, xx (1916), p. 3.
2. For the other bells mentioned, *see Accounts of the Fabric*, ii, 331. 'Salterel' seems a reasonable conjecture for the illegible S...erel; the middle letters (now missing) were read by Oliver (p. 379) as 'ok', which could easily be a mistake for 'alt'.
3. D&C 3764.
4. *Ordinale*, i, 11–12.
5. Ibid., p. 8; D&C 3550 ff. 78, 88^V, 91–^{V}; 3551 f. 52^V.
6. *Ordinale*, i, 2.
7. Ibid., pp. 6–7.
8. There are occasional grants of leave in D&C 3550–52.
9. *Ordinale*, i, 6.
10. Ibid., p. 7.

11. Ibid., p. 20. The standard work on medieval cathedral music is F. Ll. Harrison, *Music in Medieval Britain*, 2nd edn, London, 1963. *See also* N. Orme, 'The Early Musicians of Exeter Cathedral', *Music and Letters*, lix (1978), pp. 395–410.
12. *Ordinale*, i, 15–16, 20–22.
13. Oliver, p. 329.
14. *Ordinale*, i, 3, 5.
15. Ibid., p. 4.
16. Ibid., pp. 38–9.
17. D&C 3686, 2 ff. at each end.
18. *Ordinale*, i, 8–11.
19. *Reg. Grandisson*, i, 586–7.
20. *Calendar of Patent Rolls, 1317–21*, p.72.
21. *Ordinale*, i, 136.
22. D&C 3550 f. 91^V.
23. DRO, Exeter Chamber Act Book, II (12 Feb 1538); *The Chantry Certificates for Devon & Exeter*, ed. L.S. Snell, Exeter, (1961) pp. 8–9.
24. *Ordinale*, i, 18; ii, 539; D&C 3625 f. 114.
25. *Ordinale*, i, 30–33.
26. D&C 3550 f. 26.
27. Oliver, pp. 467, 475.
28. Ibid.; *Reg. Stapeldon*, p. 148.
29. John Hooker (information supplied to J. Foxe, *Acts and Monuments*, London, 1610, p. 947), suggests 5.00; D&C 3552 f. 140 says 6.00.
30. The ordinances establishing the Horsey chantry, 1531–41, mention 6.00 (D&C 2924) and those of the Speke chantry, 1518, 8.00 (D&C 2416).
31. D&C 600; Oliver, p. 417.
32. *Ordinale*, i, 35.
33. Ibid., p. 37. n.4.
34. Ibid., pp. 37–8.
35. Ibid., pp. 39–40, 293–9.
36. Ibid., p.40.
37. D&C 2367; of. 2924.
38. G. Oliver, *Monasticon Dioecesis Exoniensis*, Exeter, 1846, p. 406.
39. D&C 3625 f. 113; *Ordinale*, ii, 538.
40. Ibid., i, 40–41, 23–9.
41. *Letters of Shillingford*, ed. Moore, p. 86: Oliver, pp. 467, 475.
42. D&C 3625 f. 114; *Ordinale*, ii, 539. Curfew was at 9.00 p.m. in 1562 (Hooker, *Description*, iii, 929–30).

Chapter 8: The Year

1. *Ordinale*, ii, 539.
2. Ibid., i, 64.
3. Ibid., pp. 66–7, 303–5.
4. Ibid., ii, 539.
5. Ibid., p. 547.
6. *Reg. Grandisson*, iii, 1213–14.
7. *Ordinale*, i, 74–7.
8. H.C. Maxwell-Lyte, *A History of Eton College*, 4th edn, London, 1911, pp. 495–517.
9. Oliver, pp. 228–9.

10. *Ordinale*, i, 311–12.
11. Ibid., p. 13.
12. Ibid., pp. 317–20.
13. D&C 2781; 3773 ff. 4^V, 7^V, etc.
14. *Ordinale*, i, 136–7, 320–21.
15. Ibid., pp. 138, 322–4.
16. Ibid., pp. 138–9.
17. The procession on 25 April was not held if that day fell in Easter week or on a Sunday (*Ordinale*, pp. 221–2).
18. Ibid., pp. 317, 329, 332.
19. *The Exeter Book*, ed. Chambers, p. 49; 3625 ff.22–3; Curtis, *Disputes*, pp. 23–5; 3770 f. 202^V.
20. *See* p. 51.
21. D&C 3770 f. 202^V; Curtis, *Disputes*, p. 24.
22. *Reg. Stapeldon*, pp. 334–5.
23. *Ordinale*, i, 161, 221–2, 327, 346.
24. Ibid., i, 160–61, 327–8. The information is clarified by W.G. Henderson, *Processionale ad Usum Sarum*, Leeds, 1832, pp. 103–24, and C. Wordsworth, *Ceremonies and Processions of the Cathedral Church of Salisbury*, Cambridge, 1901, pp. 92–3. The dragon and lion were not carried on 25 April (*Ordinale*, i, 346). The significance of the dragon is explained in Jacobo da Voragine, *The Golden Legend*, trans. W. Caxton, London, 1931, i, 105–6.
25. *The Diary of Henry Machyn*, ed. J.G. Nichols, London, Camden Society, xlii (1848), pp. 61, 236; J.C. Cox, *Churchwardens' Accounts*, London, 1913, pp. 72, 263–4.
26. D&C 3773 ff. 5–51. D&C 3550 f. 47 says that they were eaten by the canons and 'officials'.
27. *Two Fifteenth-Century Cookery Books*, ed. T. Austin, London, Early English Text Society, original series, xci (1888), pp. 51, 55–6, 73.
28. *The Exeter Book*, ed. Chambers, p. 49.
29. D&C 2694, and following accounts down to 2704 (e).
30. *Reg. Grandisson*, ii, 1055–6.
31. *Calendar of State Papers Venetian*, vol. vii: *1558-1580*, p.11.

Chapter 9: The Saints

1. The relic lists are: Bodleian Library, MS Auct. D.2.16 f. 8 (printed in Sir W. Dugdale, *Monasticon Anglicanum*, ed. J. Caley et al., 6 vols in 8, London, 1817–30, ii, 528–31); MS Bodley 579 (printed in *The Leofric Missal*, ed. F.E. Warren, Oxford, 1883, pp. 3–5) and D&C 2861.
2. Rose-Troup, *Exeter Vignettes*, pp. 15–18.
3. *Ordinale*, ii, 547; Oliver, pp. 298, 311.
4. D&C 3773 ff. 5, 10.
5. D&C 3764, *passim*.
6. Oliver, pp. 352–3.
7. Chaplais in *Bulletin of the Institute of Historical Research*, xxxix (1966), p. 8.
8. *The Exeter Book*, ed. Chambers, p.49. The inferior status of St Paul to St Peter, even in the fourteenth century, can be seen in the grading of their feasts (*Ordinale*, i, 15), and in the lack of a statue to St Paul in the nave along with those of the Virgin Mary and St Peter.
9. *Reg. Grandisson*, i, 434.
10. D&C 2912 (Cross); 3672 f. 339–^{V}, 1930, and *Accounts of the Fabric*, i, 3 (St

Edmund); *Reg. Bronescombe*, p. 279 (St John 'in the nave'); D&C 1846, 1848 (St Mary 'in the nave'); 1936–7 and Oliver, pp. 426–7 (St Richard); *Accounts of the Fabric*, i, 7 (St Paul, 'north tower').

11. *Reg. Bronescombe*, pp. 38–9; D&C 343.
12. *Reg. Bronescombe*, p. 51.
13. Dr Avril Henry points out to me, however, that artists usually placed St John on the south side of the Virgin and St Gabriel on the north.
14. *Ordinale*, i, 68, 76, 221, 247.
15. *Accounts of the Fabric*, i, 2 (St James), 6 (St Mary Magdalene). A document of 1302 mentions the altar of St Mary (unspecified) and St Thomas the Martyr (i.e. Becket) near the vestry (D&C 2129). This has caused the Magdalene altar to be ascribed to Thomas, who was evidently the second dedicatee. A reference of 1431 to the statue of St Mary Magdalene standing near the vestry, together with the other evidence, clinches the dedication in her favour (*Reg. Lacy*, iv, 23).
16. The St Nicholas altar is first mentioned in 1327 (Oliver, p. 314).
17. There are references to a chapel of St Radegund in 1350–51 (*Accounts of the Fabric*, ii, 206–7), for which two explanations have been given: 1. They refer to St Radegund's chapel in Palace Gate (Lega-Weekes, *Cathedral Close*, pp. 116–21) but, against this, the Fabric Accounts do not normally deal with buildings other than the cathedral; 2. they refer to the Grandisson chapel in the cathedral, which perhaps took over the earlier altar dedication to St Radegund (*Accounts of the Fabric*, ii, p. xxxiv). The latter has more merit, given the possible location of the earlier altar in the nave of the cathedral near the later Grandisson chapel. However, Grandisson himself has left no trace of an interest in St Radegund, and his chapel is always referred to in other documents in a roundabout way without mentioning its dedication, which suggests that one was not used. So the Radegund dedication did not win acceptance and survive, since it is never again heard of.
18. *Reg. Grandisson*, i, 95.
19. Ibid., ii, 697–8.
20. Ibid., ii, 873–6.
21. *Calendar of Papal Letters*, iii: *1342–62*, p. 139.
22. D&C 3505B ff. 1, 223–4.
23. *Ordinale*, i, 240, 264, 267, 274, 276.
24. See pp. 25, 27.
25. D&C 3766 *s.a.* 1352, 1353 (where St Agnes is mentioned, probably by mistake), 1356; MS Misc. 1/2.
26. *Reg. Brantyngham*, i, 497–8.
27. *Ordinale*, i, p. xli.
28. D&C 2657; 2676; 3678 ff. 2–3; 3773 f. 54^V; 3774/fragments f.3^V.
29. *Reg. Lacy*, i, 144.
30. D&C 2678, 2683.
31. D&C 2704(a); compare 2704 (b–f).
32. *Reg. Lacy*, iv, 295.
33. On the Raphael cult, *see* Orme in *Analecta Bollandiana*, civ (1986), forthcoming.
34. N. Orme, 'Sir John Speke and his Chapel in Exeter Cathedral', *Devonshire Association Transactions*, cxviii (1986), forthcoming.
35. Alexander Barclay, *The Life of St George*, ed. W. Nelson, London, Early English Text Society, original series, ccxxx, (1955), pp. 14, 55, 60, 107.
36. D&C 2912.
37. *Reg. Brantyngham*, ii, 742.
38. N. Orme, 'The Dissolution of the Chantries in Devon', *Devonshire Association*

Transactions, cxi (1979), p. 107; Beatrix F. Cresswell, *Exeter Churches*, Exeter, 1908, p. 145.

39. *Ordinale*, i, p. xliii. *See also* R.W. Pfaff *New Liturgical Feasts in Later Medieval England*, Oxford, 1970.
40. Oliver, p. 365.
41. D&C 2413.
42. Oliver, p. 198; Public Record Office, Prob. 11/19 ff. 147^V–8 (will of Hugh Oldham).

Chapter 10: The Reformation

1. Virtually all the information about Benet comes from John Hooker, directly in Exeter City Archives, Book 51, f. 341^V, and reported to John Foxe, *Acts and Monuments*, London, 1610, pp. 946–9, where the burning is dated 15 January. *See also* G.E. Tapley-Soper, 'Thomas Benet and Master Dusgate', *Devonshire Association Transactions*, lxiii (1931), pp. 369–80.
2. Foxe, *Acts and Monuments*, pp. 946–9.
3. *Letters and Papers, Foreign and Domestic, Henry VIII*, vii, 107–8; xii part ii, 211.
4. On the vicars and annuellars in the early 16th century, *see* N. Orme in *Devonshire Association Transactions*, cxiii (1981), pp. 88–90, 98–9.
5. DRO, Exeter, Book 51, ff. 341 (Ryse), 342 (Carslegh), 345 (Weston), 346 (Parkhouse), 346^V (Tregonwell).
6. Ibid., f. 342–^{V}; compare *Letters and Papers*, vii, 177.
7. *Valor Ecclesiasticus tempore Henrici VIII*, ed. J. Caley, 6 vols, London, Record Commission, 1810–24; for Exeter Cathedral, *see* ii, 292–9.
8. Tregonwell's visitation is mentioned in 1538 as having happened earlier (*Letters and Papers*, xiii part i, 24), but evidently took place at the turn of 1535–6 (ibid., x, 1).
9. *Visitation Articles and Injunctions of the Period of the Reformation*, ed. W.H. Frere and W. McC. Kennedy, vol. ii, London, Alcuin Club, xv (1910), pp. 3–9.
10. For Pole's career, *see* A.B. Emden, *A Biographical Register of the University of Oxford A.D. 1501 to 1540*, Oxford, 1974, pp. 453–5.
11. *Letters and Papers*, xii part i, 334, 367, 516.
12. For Heynes's career, *see* the *Dictionary of National Biography* (Oxford).
13. *Letters and Papers*, xii part ii, 60.
14. D&C 3552 f. 1.
15. *Letters and Papers*, xxi part ii, 211.
16. D&C 3552 ff. 1^V–7.
17. *Visitation Articles*, ed. Frere and Kennedy, ii, 37–8.
18. *Tudor Royal Proclamations*, ed. P.L. Hughes and J.F. Larkin, vol. i, New Haven and London, 1964, pp. 275–6.
19. D&C 3552 ff. 14^V–15^V.
20. British Library, Harley MS 604 ff. 164–7^V, printed in Oliver, pp. 477–83.
21. D&C 3552 ff. 11, 14.
22. Ibid., ff. 14^V–15^V.
23. Ibid., f. 20.
24. *Letters and Papers*, xviii part i, 158, 160, 167, 176, 267, 299, 461; *Acts of the Privy Council of England*, new series, vol. i, *1542–7*, ed. J.R. Dasent, London 1890, pp. 97–8, 117, 126, 150–51.
25. There are two visitation documents of 1547; one giving orders to all cathedrals (D&C 3764 pp. 28–35, also printed in *Visitation Articles*, ed. Frere and

Kennedy, ii, 135–9), and the other giving additional orders to Exeter alone (D&C 3764 pp. 50–61).

26. Orme, *Education in the West of England*, pp. 54–5.
27. Orme in *Devonshire Association Transactions*, cxiii (1981), pp. 99–100.
28. For the best text of the 1549 prayer-book, *see* F.E. Brightman, *The English Rite*, 2nd edn, 2 vols, London 1921.
29. E. Cardwell, *Documentary Annals of the Reformed Church of England*, new edn, 2 vols, London, 1894, i, 45–6.
30. *Tudor Royal Proclamations*, ed. Hughes & Larkin, i, 302.
31. D&C 3552, f. 140.
32. H.F. Fulford Williams, 'The Vestments of Bishop Grandisson now in the Azores', *Devonshire Association Transactions*, xciv (1962), pp. 613–22.
33. Donne, *Holy Sonnets*, no. 18.
34. His presence is recorded only once after 1547, on 5 August 1550 (D&C 3552 f. 46–^{v}).
35. For Heynes's will, *see* Public Record Office, Prob. 11/35 ff. 228–30 (PCC 29 Powell).

Appendix 1
A note on the plan of the Norman cathedral

Our knowledge of the plan of the Norman cathedral is incomplete, and reconstructions are highly conjectural, pending more archaeological discoveries. Two plans have been proposed: by W.R. Lethaby, 'How Exeter Cathedral was Built', *Architectural Review*, xiii (1907), pp. 167–76, adopted in Bishop and Prideaux, *The Building of Exeter Cathedral*, figure 1, and by C.A.R. Radford, 'The Romanesque Cathedral at Exeter' *Friends of Exeter Cathedral, 30th Annual Report* (1960), pp. 28–36. My own plan is based on both of these, modified by the documentary evidence about the use of the Norman building and its successor in the thirteenth and fourteenth centuries — evidence which has not been considered hitherto.

1. It seems best to imagine the east end without apsidal chapels. If such chapels had existed, one would expect their altar dedications to have survived into the Decorated cathedral. The latter had two eastern chapels of St John the Evangelist and St Gabriel, but they were not dedicated to saints when they were first built, and seem to enshrine new cults (*Accounts of the Fabric*, ii, pp. xxvii, 317–18). This makes unlikely earlier dedications and therefore chapels.

2. No structural or documentary evidence survives for eastern bays in the north and south towers before the construction of the chapels of St Paul and St John in the 1280s (V. Hope and L.J. Lloyd, *Exeter Cathedral*, Exeter, 1973, p. 6). Mr J. Allan points out to me that the towers, until the 1280s, were primarily towers and not transepts.

3. The building of an asymmetrical chapel of St Edmund at the north-west corner of the Decorated cathedral, superfluous to its plan, suggests a desire to accommodate an earlier altar and saint-cult on this site. The altar of St Edmund existed as far back as 1263 and was important, being served by at least two chantry priests (D&C 3672 f. 339–^{V}; 1930). On liturgical grounds, we must therefore postulate some kind of bay at this spot in the Norman cathedral to hold the altar, and (for symmetry) another at the opposite south-west corner. The latter could have included the altar of St Richard and St Radegund (mentioned below). The bays on the plan are intended symbolically to make this liturgical point; their dimensions may have been different.

4. A number of altars are mentioned in the Norman cathedral in the thirteenth century (for references, *see* Chapter 9, note 10). It is not absolutely clear where they stood, and the locations suggested here are likely but not certain. The Lady chapel, first recorded in 1236 (D&C 600), could have been in the south tower, for the reason explained below in relation to St John the Baptist. The altars of the Cross, St Paul, St Mary (nave) and St Edmund were presumably in similar positions in the Norman cathedral that they occupied in the Decorated one. The altar of St John the Baptist was in the nave in 1271 (Oliver, pp. 422–3), and an undated thirteenth-century deed which also locates it in the nave seems to link it with the altar of St Mary (D&C 231). A place beside St Mary's altar in front of the choir-screen is likely for such an important saint. By 1285, however, the cult of St John the Baptist had been moved to the altar in the south tower (*Accounts of the Fabric*, i, 6; compare D&C 3675 f. 57), and the nave altar was eventually rededicated to St Nicholas. This move coincides with the transference of the Lady chapel to a new building at the east end, and raises the possibility that it had been previously housed in the south tower. That leaves the altar of St Richard and St Radegund to be located in the south-west corner of the nave. Such an arrangement would explain the apparent transference of the Radegund dedication to the Grandisson chapel near by (discussed in Chapter 9, note 17).

116

Appendix 2
A note on the Black Death

The Black Death (or plague) reached England in the summer of 1348, and caused great loss of life in the following twelve months or so. About ten of the twenty-four canons of Exeter Cathedral died in 1348–9, most of them from the plague, including the chancellor, Thomas Buckingham, a notable theologian (Le Neve, *Fasti*, ed. Horn, pp. 24–34). Less is known about the minor clergy, but at least five vicars choral and annuellars died, and probably several more (Orme in *Devonshire Association Transactions*, cxiii (1981), pp. 84–5, 93–5). Cathedral life, however, was not totally disrupted. Lay people continued to make offerings of money at about the usual level (D&C 3766), and the cathedral workmen went on doing maintenance tasks (*Accounts of the Fabric*, ii, p. xxxiv).

The damage of the plague was long-term as much as immediate. Although the vacant canonries were soon filled up, it proved impossible to make good the losses among the minor clergy. Up to 1348 there were large numbers of clergy in England, and men could be recruited to take up the rather poorly paid work of vicars choral and annuellars. After 1348 there were fewer clergy, and it was easier for them to get more attractive posts as rectors or vicars of parishes. The number of vicars choral at Exeter accordingly dropped from twenty-four to twenty, and that of the annuellars from twenty-one to twelve. With fewer clergy working in the cathedral, plans to build more altars had to be abandoned, and two chapels — that of St Edmund and the charnel chapel — ceased to be served by clergy at all. The first outbreak of the plague was followed by others, and it was not until the 1370s and 1380s that the recruitment of minor clergy improved and the life of the building began to return to the level of the early 1340s (Orme in *Devonshire Association Transactions*, cited above).

Index

118